BORN INTO MADNESS:
WHEN THOSE WHO ARE SUPPOSED TO LOVE YOU CAN'T

Born Into Madness:
When Those Who Are Supposed To Love You Can't

KAREN R. KAISER, PH.D.

Design Grade Design and Adeline Media, London

Author's Note *This book is nonfiction. Where applicable, names, distinguishing traits, and other identifying characteristics of the individuals described here have been changed in order to protect their privacy.*

First print April 2020

ISBN 978-0-9995901-9-5

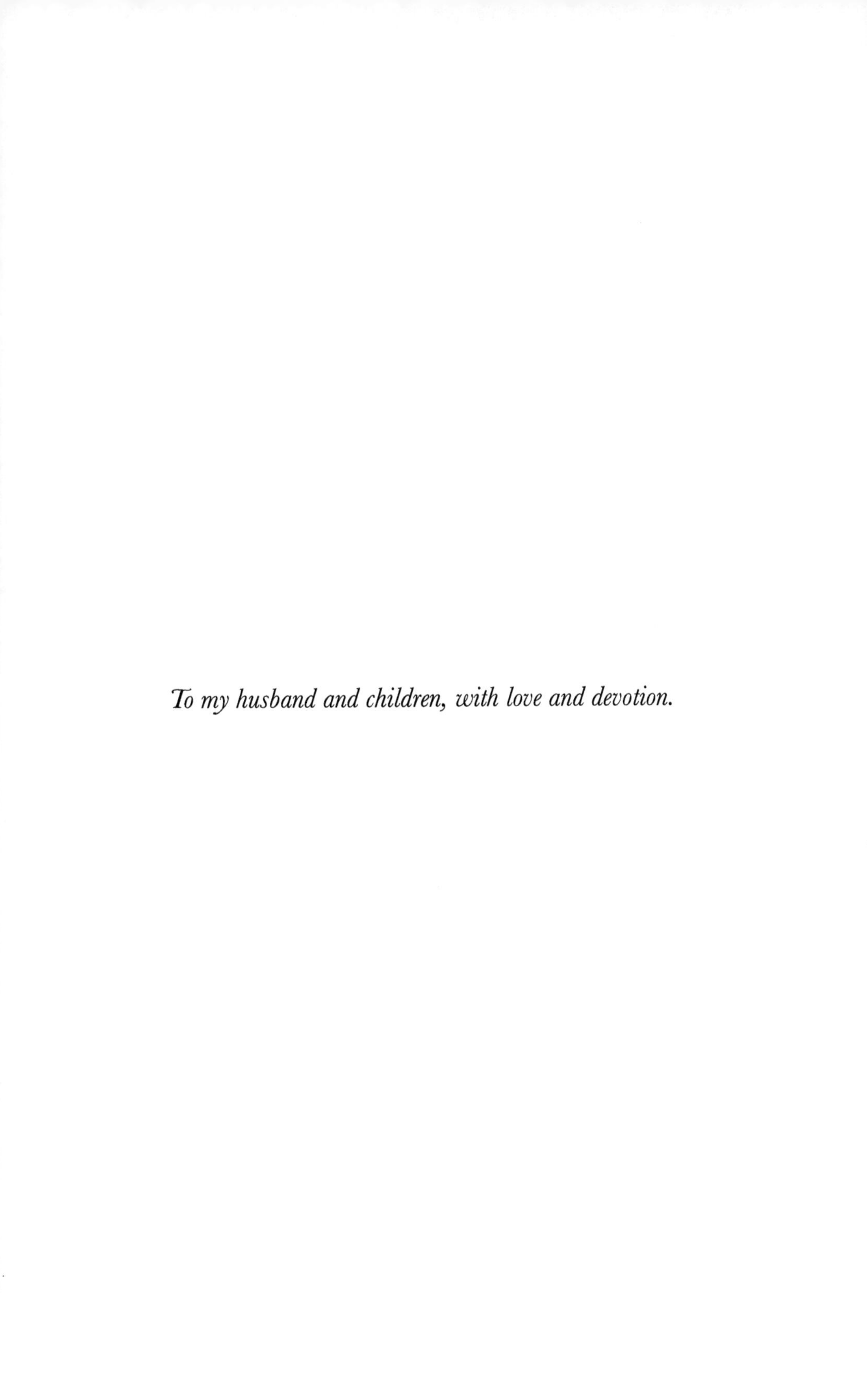

To my husband and children, with love and devotion.

CONTENTS

PROLOGUE

B*orn Into Madness* chronicles my family's intense struggle living in multiple realities and their journey to find a way forward in the face of generational illnesses that continue to disrupt and pull us into chaos and torment.

I was born into madness. I watched my family's demise, desperately searching for answers about why every member of my immediate family was becoming increasingly insane, a shadow of their former selves. They would return only to leave again, until finally, they never returned.

And now, the illnesses are at my children's door. And I am desperate to save them. My children didn't ask to be here. But here they are. My lifelong search for answers has brought me full circle, to the beginning, to where it all began. The answers were there all along, some buried in my subconscious, and some answers embedded in the workings of our family system.

1

LOVE THY MOTHER

Honor your father and your mother, so that
you may live long in the land of the
Lord your God is giving you.

–*Exodus 20:3 New International Version*

Death can make you reexamine the course of your life: decisions made; events, past and present; and your relationships, particularly with the deceased.

That's what happened to me. As I was writing my mother's memorial after her death, I searched for something good to say about her. The experience made me wonder: *Did I love my mother?* Looking back on the turbulent years of my life, I was forced to search for an identity separate from my mother and father—an identity that I could live with.

On the day of my mother's death, I woke up to a phone call from the nursing home.

"Mrs. Kaiser, this is Nurse Joniah from Dr. Lee's office. I am here at Baker's Pavilion with your mother, and the nurse on duty phoned our office early this morning stating that they couldn't get vitals on your mom."

"What does that mean?" I asked.

"They weren't able to feel your mother's pulse, but I have been able to detect a faint one. Do you live nearby?"

I told her that I lived only eight miles from the nursing home.

"You should come as soon as you can."

Feeling the weight of yet another crisis, I got into motion. At this point, my mother had been in a near vegetative state for years. She had two strokes and had been diagnosed with normal pressure hydrocephalus ten years earlier. Was this another stroke, or perhaps an effect of the hydrocephalus? My mind grasped at straws, trying to find context for the ensuing crisis. I asked myself: *How does someone so broken live so long?*

When I arrived at my mother's bedside with Stephen (my husband) and our children (Brian and Maria), we found her lying on her back with a pillow placed under her head and bed covers pulled up to her chest. Her fine gray hair was neatly brushed back from her face. Her face was entirely free of wrinkles because of the excess fluid that had been collecting in her body for so long. She lay motionless, as if she wasn't even alive, but we could see that she was quietly moving air with shallow breaths.

We sat with her all the rest of that day, reflecting, remembering and reading the same Bible verses that she had read to me and my siblings, Marie and Danny, decades ago. *I need to do the right things for her so that I can live with myself,* I thought, but I felt numb as I looked at my mother, devoid of anger, hurt, or even sadness.

The chief nurse checked in from time to time and assessed my mother's worsening condition. She showed us the necrosis creeping up my mother's feet and legs, a sign that her circulation was slowly failing; death was finally taking her.

Hours went by. My mother seemed to be living for us, one shallow breath after another. She didn't move, and her hands were frozen in place. I pushed through a few more Bible verses, as I believed a dutiful daughter should. I didn't want my actions to be guided by the resentments that I had harbored for most of my life.

That day, I was able to carry out my responsibilities as my mother's only available child. The stillness of those moments was broken by the footsteps of the hospice chaplain who came to pray with our family. She was a tall woman with a soft voice; we could hear in her kind words that she wanted to give us the peace we needed. Of all that she said, I remember most my father's favorite Bible verse, Psalm 23:4:

Even though I walk through the valley of the shadow of death, I will fear no evil: for you are with me; your rod and your staff they comfort me. (New American Standard Bible).

It was past midnight when I realized that my mother was waiting for us to leave so that she could take her own leave. Always a private person, she likely wanted to die without anyone at her side, holding onto her earthly body.

Stephen and I left her bedside and drove home. Around 2:30 in the morning, my phone rang. It was the nursing home. My mother had been wanting to die for many years, and now, she had finally found peace. I thought about the teachings of my great-grandmother and the family church and hoped that my mother had received forgiveness, that she was in heaven with her mother and her mother's mother.

2

TARRYING FOR THE HOLY GHOST

And, behold, I send the promise of my Father upon you: but TARRY ye in the city of Jerusalem, until ye be endued with power from on high.
–Luke 24:49 King James Version

My maternal great-grandmother, Sister Mary Ruth Poindexter, was a strong-willed woman. She had seven children and left her husband, who beat her. At one point, she lived in Washington, D.C. When she moved back to Virginia, she watched white children and washed clothes for a living. At that time, the family was very poor—so poor that they had to be creative and come up with many ways to eat beans, the food staple available to them. My great-grandmother kept a garden and had her children search the house for pennies to buy food. Eventually, she was able to buy two houses in Roanoke on Route 29 with her earnings.

My mother's own mother had died during childbirth when she was eighteen, at which point her husband, my grandfather Carter, disappeared. This is how it came to be that my mother was raised by her grandmother.

My great-grandmother was one of the few people who showed me love while I was growing up. Her house became a refuge, especially when things were difficult to bear in my own home. Each Sunday, she had a big dinner for the whole family. And every summer, I had the joy of spending the long summer days with her.

Like most children, I loved summertime. As soon as school let out, Marie, Danny, and I headed to Roanoke, Virginia to be with Grandma.

By the time we were born, my great-grandmother's financial circumstances had improved. She moved into a large home with two fireplaces and a spacious yard. Her home was amazingly cozy given the size. We children mostly spent our time around the kitchen table, talking and laughing while Grandma prepared large meals of fried chicken, potato salad, green beans, peach cobbler, warm, soft rolls, and sweet tea. Grandma would slice fresh tomatoes from her garden that we ate, sprinkled with sugar. These meals were shared with our cousins, other family members, neighbors, and church members who randomly dropped by. At Grandma's house, her fellow church members were like family. The house filled with family and friends as the summer evenings went on.

Visiting Grandma meant attending church services as many as five times a week. Sometimes, we'd go to church early in the morning and stay until 3:00 in the afternoon!

For both of my parents, the Apostolic Church was a huge part of their lives and their families'; it's where they met. The Apostolic Church is a very restrictive religion, not much different from the Muslim faith. Women are not allowed to wear makeup, shorts, pants, or jewelry. They can't show any part of their body, and they wear plain dresses with long sleeves that they made themselves.

Grandma wasn't always religious. When she was in her fifties, she was diagnosed with stage four stomach cancer, a terminal diagnosis. Her doctors told her there was nothing else they could do for her and sent her home to die, with a ghastly open sore protruding from her abdomen.

Grandma wanted to be baptized prior to her death. At the First Church of Christ, she was wrapped in a sheet and lowered into the baptismal pool. After her baptism, the elders of the church visited her daily to pray with her. Incredibly, the sore healed, and my grandmother's cancer miraculously remitted. Despite the fatal diagnosis, Grandma would live another 40 years.

My family and the church considered her healing a miracle, and rightfully so. Afterwards, our family was faithful to the First Church of Christ. We were true believers in the teachings of the church. Non-believers became the "others."

Attending church was a big part of spending time with Grandma. These were not ordinary church services, mind you, but lengthy, charismatic services. The services began normally enough with the reading of scripture and quiet prayer, but as the services progressed, so did the energy and fervor of the church.

One evening, when I was about five or six, I witnessed something that I'd never seen before: church members tarrying for the Holy Ghost.

Elder Coleman, a senior church member, called church members to gather around the altar; the members obediently left their pews and walked solemnly to the altar at the front of the church. Elder Coleman led them in the chant.

"Jesus, Jesus, Jesus"

"Jesus, Jesus, Jesus"

"Jesus, Jesus, Jesus."

I watched from the pew in amazement. The floor vibrated as parishioners began stomping the floor. Heads nodding faster and faster, white spittle coming from mouths.

"Jesus, Jesus, Jesus"

"Jesus, Jesus, Jesus"

"Jesus, Jesus, Jesus."

The church seemed to have a heartbeat.

As they were caught up in the rhythm, the Holy Spirit entering their bodies, they began to speak in a different language, one that I didn't understand.

"Mmm shama lama."

"Shat a ba, shaya, shaya, shaya."

"Thank you, Lord."

"Mighty God."

"Sha bara roso sattatata."

"Dukuwnana, o rabba shabba."

The worship went on late into the evening. The church became intensely alive with the Holy Ghost. People were swaying to and fro, chanting, flailing, convulsing, and even falling to the floor. Eventually, out of exhaustion, church members became quieter, but still, there were occasional outbursts of "Thank you Jesus!" followed by sudden jerks and convulsions as the members smoldered with sanctified feelings.

Elder Coleman finally brought the spectacular service to a close with Bible quotes and cautioning remarks to beware the enemy—the "other."

I sat eyes wide in total amazement at what I had witnessed that evening. I went to church with my parents but only on Sundays, and the congregation didn't tarry on Sundays. I wondered, *what happened? What was this?* Later, I would learn that other churches danced with poisonous snakes. When I got older, I brought a boyfriend to church, and he became very frightened when he witnessed tarrying for the first time. I can understand why.

Although the church was very restrictive, this worked for many members of the congregation. The pastor told people how to live and what to do, which was exactly what some people needed. I remember seeing new people show up to church looking filthy and with their belongings in bags. Over time, with the help of the church, they became strong and healthy. They got good jobs and became functioning members of society.

In my family, my own parents began moving away from the church. My mother's mental health problems made it hard for her to function. As my father became more successful, he got too big for his britches, in the eyes of the church. When he opened a nightclub, that was the last straw; I was around ten years old when the pastor called my father a sinner in church and kicked us out of the congregation. And so began the downfall of our family.

Throughout my childhood, I witnessed many horrible things at the hands of my parents, and I'd wonder to myself: *Where is my church's God now? If there is a God, why is this happening?*

3

THE ONES WHO ARE SUPPOSED TO LOVE YOU

"And what if – what are you if the people who are supposed to love you can leave you like you're nothing"

–Scott, 2010, p. 169

I woke to the sounds of a baby crying. It was Danny, and he was screaming.

"Why won't Mom pick him up?" I whispered to my sister, Marie.

He seemed to cry forever. Marie and I dared not move. We had already seen what our father was capable of; we'd been exposed to his explosive tendencies all our lives.

The darkness erupted with heated commotion as we heard my father screaming at my mother to pick up the baby. "You pick him up!" my mother screamed back.

Marie and I listened from our bedroom; our faces stricken with fear as we heard our father fly into a fit of rage. From the sounds that night, we deduced that he'd jumped on my mother and was beating her in the head and face. Suddenly, there was a loud thud as the bed broke, falling to the ground.

My father cursed and jumped out of the bed, grabbing Danny. Later, my mother told me that he put a pillow over Danny's face and smothered the baby until he stopped crying.

"Danny didn't deserve that," my mother lamented. "Poor little boy."

I don't know if my father smothered Danny with a pillow that night. Somehow, though, Danny did stop crying. The next morning, my mother was covered in bruises, but Danny seemed alright. I thought to myself: *I live with monsters.*

If only it were that simple! If only I could just call *them* monsters and be done with it—be done with them.

My father was a violent drunk and a chronically hypomanic narcissist. He could work and party 24/7 with little need for sleep. He made a lot of money, and he spent every dime of his earnings. He lived well beyond his means, wearing tailored suits and smoking expensive cigars. He was a man who loved expensive cars, liquor, and women. He used people as he would a piece of tissue. However, like my mother, there was a different side to my father.

My father was also a family man, the second child born in a family of twelve surviving children. My grandfather Williams was half Indian and half white. He was a lot older than my grandmother; according to the census, she was sixteen when she got pregnant for the first time, but the family says she was much younger—only thirteen years old. My grandparents' oldest child, my uncle, was disabled, likely due to a failed coat hanger abortion. My great-grandmother had tried to pierce my grandmother's uterus with a coat hanger to allow fluid to escape the womb. She then had my grandmother sit in scalding hot water. The attempted abortions failed. My oldest uncle was born with an intellectual disability and epilepsy. She went on to have twelve live births, including two sets of twins.

Even though my father was the second child, he became the "oldest" and helped his mother raise the children. The family lived in extreme poverty, and the children walked to school with holes in their shoes and without coats. My grandfather was a severe alcoholic, and, during one particularly bad bender, he drove his car into the lake. Because my grandfather was light enough to pass as white, he never wanted to be seen with his darker-skinned wife. They never went out in public together except to church.

As a child, my paternal grandparents were not kind to me. They were ashamed of my dark skin and kept me cloistered at home. My sister, Marie, on the other hand, got taken out to the dime store and such. I couldn't stand my grandmother; she always said that my hair was too hard to comb, and that's why they wouldn't take me out, but I knew the truth. During one visit, one of my uncles pulled out his penis and tried to get us to touch it. I told my mother, and that was one of the last times we ever were with the Williams family.

My father was raised in poverty to uneducated parents. His relatives who hadn't been slaves had been farmers. Some had their own land and even owned slaves. Still, my father was able to get himself to college. He attended Hampton on a football scholarship but dropped out after a year; apparently, he didn't want to get hurt. After returning home from college, he worked in manufacturing for a short while and then started a small cleaning company that he grew to a large commercial cleaning company. Next, he opened a nightclub and a used car lot. He employed his nine brothers and two sisters, making sure they, as well as his parents, were taken care of financially.

Like my mother, my father began life humbly with good intentions, but something went terribly wrong. My father lost his way and got caught up in a world of lying, cheating, adultery, and excessive drinking.

As a child, I developed a love for animals early on. We lived in the country next to my great-grandfather, who had acres of uncultivated land, which served as our expansive playground where we could run freely and interact with the wildlife. Much to my mother's horror, I loved catching birds in the backyard and presenting them to her as presents. Along with my sister, brother, and cousins, I walked barefoot in the creek, using abandoned jars and jugs left by squatters to catch frogs, tadpoles, crawfish, and small fish. We played with feral kittens, turtles, and baby opossum. We were wild children exploring the natural world.

When I was about seven years old, I was delighted when my father bought us our first real pet—a puppy. The puppy was a Border Collie, and my mother named him Biyo because of his black-and-white coat.

"B-I-Y-O..." my mother sang to the tune of the Bingo song.

"B-I-Y-O, B-I-Y-O, B-I-Y-O, and Biyo was his name-O!"

Unfortunately, my parents should never have owned an animal. They didn't believe in having animals in the house, so my father built Biyo a doghouse and a small kennel in the yard. Biyo lived outside no matter the weather: rain, severe summer heat, and cold, snowy nights. He never came inside. Sometimes, when my parents were low on money, Biyo lived without food or water.

Even though I was just a kid, I knew that the way Biyo was being treated was wrong. So, I assumed the responsibility of caring for Biyo and all our pets early on. Doing the best a seven-year-old could, I snuck food out to his kennel and filled his water bowl. As Biyo grew bigger and bigger, he ran in circles inside the little fenced area, barking wildly. Sometimes he escaped from his kennel and got into the trash—as dogs have been known to do. One day, we came home from school, and Biyo was running through the yard with a brown bag in his mouth. The yard was covered in garbage and trash.

"Biyo, what have you done?" we all yelled. Unfortunately, my father came home seconds later, and he was in one of his dark moods. He accelerated into the driveway and swung the car door open before even reaching a full stop. My heart quickened as I watched the scene. I knew this wasn't going to end well.

"What the hell!" my father screamed and stomped over to Biyo, quickly grabbing him by the scruff of his neck. Grabbing a nearby garden hose, my father began beating Biyo violently.

Biyo yelped and writhed, panting as he tried to escape my father. Finally, he was still. As this transpired, Marie and Danny ran inside. I was frozen in horror… a horror that never left me. I couldn't move. Tears ran down my face, and my father stomped inside, ordering everyone to pick up the trash scattered around the house and driveway. How horrible a person to commit such a violent act and then order us, the children, to pick up the trash. At that moment, I truly hated my father. I hated my mother. And, I even hated God.

Since then, I've never been able to watch animal movies or even commercials with animals; I have to change the channel. The memory of Biyo always comes to my mind. I have no idea what happened to our beloved dog's body, but I think that my father finally shot him in the back of the head to finish him off. From such a young age, I was discovering that the world was full of monsters, and some of them lived in my own house. Afterwards, I always feared that, one day, my father would snap and kill us all.

It wasn't only Biyo who suffered my father's wrath. In our house, we experienced violence of some kind almost every day. As a child, I had nightmares that he would kill us in the middle of the night. One time, he thought us kids had broken a typewriter, and he came after us, throwing us across the room. He was particularly violent against Danny and my mother. In one incident, he broke a chair over my mother's back and another over the countertop, where we were all hiding on the floor underneath. Another time, he hit my brother Danny so hard that a nail came out of the wall. It was horrific to witness.

One night, when I was very young, I heard my mother grumbling from my parents' bedroom, followed by loud noises, shouts, and thrashing. "I don't feel like it," I heard my mother scream.

Then there was the sound of the backboard of my parents' bed hitting the wall and my father's moans, followed by silence. A few minutes later, I heard my mother go to the bathroom, sniffling as she walked. The next morning, her face was swollen and bruised, her nightgown torn. It was her favorite nightgown—a flowing chiffon orange gown, now with a large tear down the front. That day, my mother got up only to use the bathroom, returning to bed for the entirety of the day, and the next day, and the next...

As I got older, I began to understand a bit more about the violence that was going on behind my parent's bedroom door. One night again, we heard our father severely beating our mother. We heard what must have been her limp, bruised body hitting the door over and over again. It was terrifying. We thought he'd come after us, the kids.

The next morning, my mother emerged from the bedroom horribly bruised and left the house. She looked disturbed, walking down the street in her sullied nightgown holding a polka dot umbrella. She was gone for two weeks, living in a friend's basement. In the meantime, my father combed our hair and made our meals. Eventually, my great-grandmother convinced my mother to come back home by convincing our father to stop beating her. When she returned, she smelled like moth balls.

Soon after, my father moved our family into an upper-class white neighborhood where we lived much closer to our neighbors; perhaps this proximity to others slowed my father's violent rampage. He mostly stopped beating her after that, although one day, when my mother refused to comb my younger sister Cara's hair, he punched her in the mouth, damaging her two front teeth.

My father was extremely controlling, always keeping my mother and our family isolated. My father bought the groceries and controlled every facet of our life. Living out in the suburbs meant we were far from the city. We never lived on a bus line, and he prohibited my mother from driving. This way, he limited her social life. She maintained her friendships over the phone, speaking daily to her friend Judy and my father's sisters, who were very beautiful and very vain—just like my mother.

On the other hand, my father was a smart and successful black man in a world that didn't accept black people. We always lived in all-white communities. I was eleven when we moved into a wealthy golf course community, where we lived between two country clubs. Unfortunately, as African Americans, we weren't allowed in either one.

My father had explosive and violent tendencies, but he was also a devoted family man. We'd all rush to the door when he came home from work. Sometimes he arrived bearing gifts and candies; other times, he was in one of his moods, and we did our best to keep a safe distance. My father was bigger than life, an unusual individual with a personality that contained both lightness and darkness, good and evil.

4

GROUNDS FOR SUICIDE

They tell us that suicide is the greatest piece of cowardice... that suicide is wrong...
when it is quite obvious that there is nothing in the world
to which every man has a more unassailable
title than to his own life and person

–Schopenhauer, n.d.

Growing up, I adored my mother. She was beautiful and smelled like roses. Always delicate, she weighed a mere 99 pounds after the birth of her three children and wore pink daily. Like a dutiful mother out of a commercial, she baked homemade cakes, allowing us to scoop cake batter from the bowl after the cake pans were filled. She made matching clothes for us and read to us daily. Every day, she made sure the four of us ate all our meals together at the kitchen table, even if my father was a frequent no-show. She took us to the public library and let us select books that she would read aloud to us after dinner. She read us

Bible stories and taught us the difference between right and wrong.

But there was something inconsistent about her personality. Sometimes she was the life of the party, always ready to have a good time. During these times, which I now understand as hypomanic episodes, she was extremely productive, sewing curtains and clothes with swift rapidity. On the other hand, there were other moments when she was much demurrer and quieter, to the point of not getting out of bed for days on end. During those dark periods, she wouldn't clean the house or even feed us, her children.

As a child, it was impossible to recognize what was going on, but as an adult, I understand that my mother suffered from bipolar disorder. This explains the many ups and downs in our mother's personality that we endured as children. I believe that she became ill during her pregnancy with me. I can remember watching her respond to hallucinations when I was a little girl. It was terrifying to witness my own mother behave in such a way.

One day, when I was around six years old, I overheard a conversation between my mom and her best friend, Judy.

"He is such a dreamboat," my mother said, cackling and stomping the kitchen floor between fits of laughter. Judy was speaking so loudly that it was as if she were in the room with us.

"Did he kiss you, Eleanor?" Judy asked my mother.

"Maybe..." my mother replied, screaming with laughter.

"Dr. Powell is a good-looking man," Judy screeched.

It was like watching a performance, designed to entertain themselves. Their laughter was contagious, and I started to laugh, too, although I wasn't sure what I was laughing about. Who were they talking about? What was going on? The situation seemed light and funny, so why did I have an uneasy feeling in the pit of my stomach?

Later, my mother's dreamboat, Dr. Powell, became her rapist. Dr. Powell was her gynecologist, and, according to my mother, every time she needed to get a prescription for birth control pills, he'd hold her down and force himself on her. She accused him of "tearing her insides."

Over time, Dr. Powell became her tormentor, sending her messages through the radio and television that summoned her to meet him. Often, the messages told her to meet him at a local grocery store. She would stand in the grocery store aisles talking aloud to him, but he wasn't there—or was he? She believed he was. I watched in fear as my mother stood in front of the video cameras, believing that Dr. Powell could see and hear her. "Why won't you come out?" my mother crowed. "I know you're back there."

There were times when my mother did run into her gynecologist at the grocery store. During those occasions, she would flirt with him in a suggestive way that only held meaning for her.

"Eleanor, how are you today?"

"Fine, Dr. Powell. I've been thinking about the last time we were together. When should I come back?"

Dr. Powell looked at my mother quizzically. "Just give the office a call and ask Dorothy when your next appointment is."

"I will!" she responded with a bright smile.

These chance encounters gave my mother more impetus to go to the grocery store in search of Dr. Powell. And so, she went to the store day and night at all hours. When my mother didn't see him, she became angry and accusatory. Surely, he wasn't staying away from Eleanor on his own. She developed the belief that "people" were trying to keep her and Dr. Powell apart. During late night visits to the store, she shouted angrily at the cameras: "You can't keep us from seeing one another!" The few store employees who witnessed my mother's tirades laughed but left her to her own devices. She seemed harmless enough.

I was already 29 years old when she told me that the doctor had raped her. Still, she wanted him to leave his wife to be with her. I gave him a call, which infuriated my mother. He sounded warm and grandfatherly over the phone but expressed concern about my mother's well-being. Soon, she received a letter from his office firing her as a patient. Although my mother had been beautiful in her youth, she had become overweight over the years and had very poor hygiene. Her hair was dyed bright red, and she rarely left her bed.

I have never found out the truth about the situation. Perhaps the doctor did have sex with her, or perhaps my mother misinterpreted the gynecological exam during one of her psychotic episodes. Her mania could have led to hyper-sexual behavior, and it's possible that the doctor took advantage of the situation.

My mother's behavior was baffling and scary throughout my childhood. One early winter morning when I was very young, Marie, Danny, and I were playing in the hallway of our small, three-bedroom rambler on the outskirts of Roanoke, Virginia. We had just gotten up and were still dressed in our matching footed pajamas. We often played in the hallway as small children, sliding on the floor in our socks after the wood was freshly waxed or riding atop our toy fire trucks—our favorite Christmas presents from Santa. Each of us had received a bright red super-sized fire engine under the tree that year.

The hallway was great, because it connected every room in the house—the bathroom, living room, three bedrooms, and kitchen. We were close to our mother and all the action.

Suddenly, my mother emerged from the bedroom and stepped into the bathroom. She looked ragged and off, but I didn't know why.

"Well, I woke up this morning," my mother stated dully, staring at herself strangely in the mirror. Then, the phone rang. Marie picked up the call and handed the phone to my mother, who was still in the bathroom, moving slowly. It was Judy, my mother's best friend.

"Eleanor, what did you do?"

"I took all of the medicine in the cabinet," she responded matter-of-factly.

"Eleanor, why? Are you alright?"

"I woke up." My mother responded as if it didn't matter whether she awoke or not… whether she was OK or not. She responded as if nothing mattered.

"Eleanor, I'll be right there… I'm on my way now!"

Judy showed up not ten minutes later in tears. My mother remained calm, as if nothing had happened. I remember Judy calling my father while my mother went to sit absently on my parents' bed. We children were so young; we had no idea what was going on, so we just kept on playing. Eventually, we were taken to my great-grandmother's house. It wasn't until I was an adult that I understood the truth of this dark morning. We were innocents bearing witness to my mother's attempt to die with no regard for her three small children's fates. This would be the first of several suicide attempts by my mother.

It is difficult reconciling my early memories of Mom. On one hand, she was exactly what you would want a mother to be: caring, loving, diligent regarding our welfare, actively engaging with us daily. On the other hand, she could be bitter, selfish, and angry, especially when she was in a mixed state of mania and depression. She picked on me relentlessly, veiling nasty comments, but I was too young to understand that I was being tortured.

What led my mother to attempt suicide? I cannot say for certain. She was in her early twenties, isolated in the suburbs with three small children, and a victim of domestic violence. She didn't finish high school. She dropped out in ninth grade to marry my father. It's very likely that she felt extremely trapped. My father often came home late, if he came home at all. When he did come home, he smelled of cigars and liquor. He was either full of bravado—bigger than life—or irritable and explosive. The four of us (my siblings and our mother) tiptoed around him until we knew which version of our father had come home. This couldn't have been the life she'd dreamed of.

5

BEWARE THE COMPANY YOU KEEP

Power tends to corrupt, and absolute power corrupts absolutely. Great men are almost always bad men.

–Acton, 1887

I do not sit with deceitful men, nor will I go with pretenders. I hate the assembly of evildoers, And I will not sit with the wicked.

–Psalm 26:4-5 New American Standard Version

Many descriptors apply to my father. There was a recklessness and dangerousness that ran through him—a devil may care, live-for-today kind of attitude. He did amoral things without consciousness about his actions. He was a complex character, and being his daughter meant that I was along for one hell of a ride… literally.

On weekends, my father drove us around to visit other family members. We played a lot of sports and did a lot of activities with his brothers and their children, including an annual Williams family Easter egg hunt. Sometimes, we went to the movies as a family.

But as fun as these activities were, being in a car with my father behind the wheel was always a terrifying experience. The way he drove was symbolic of the roller coaster that was my father's life. I squeezed Marie's hand as my father sped through turns and ran stop lights, the car lifting from the ground as it bounced airborne down the hills of Roanoke leading to the bed of the James River. Too afraid to utter a sigh, I sat petrified, screaming on the inside. If anyone dared let out a peep, my father, who had a long reach, could soundly slap any one of us without even turning around.

I had a recurring dream for many years, from early childhood through late adolescence—although perhaps it's best described as a nightmare. In it, I was alone late at night sitting in the back seat of a 1969 limelight green Firebird hurtling down 12th Street. My drive down the street started slowly enough, but as the street sloped steeper and steeper, the car speed incrementally increased. The car sped out of control heading for the downtown train tracks, and, ultimately, the James River.

I had this nightmare night after night and woke up sweating and gasping for air, so frightened out of my skin that I didn't want to go back to sleep.

The dream continued until, one day, I realized that I just needed to push the car brakes to stop the car. The problem was that I was too small to reach the brakes; to make matters worse, I was sitting in the back seat. It took many years before I could finally climb from the back seat over into the driver's seat by sliding forward on my stomach towards the brake pedal. Pushing the brake pedal down to the floor, I woke up in a rushing sense of relief. Some evenings, I would almost wake prior to reaching the pedal, but I willed myself to reach the brakes before my eyes opened.

My father was a businessman, and his work kept him busy day and night. He was gone all the time, and we assumed he was hard at work. He owned multiple businesses, including a nightclub, a cleaning company, and a car lot where he sold cars that he'd bought at auction and restored. You could find my father in the early morning, working underneath a car that he was fixing to sell. My father got a brand-new Lincoln or Mercedes every year, and when we were old enough to drive, we were given cars, too. Oddly enough, my father had a bedroom in each of his offices; the bedroom at the top of his nightclub included a bed with a heart-shaped velvet red headboard.

He was known to carry around thousands of dollars in cash—along with a gun for protection. I can remember him bringing home briefcases full of money and counting bills on the kitchen table; this was his payroll process. He thought of himself as John Shaft, a fictional private investigator and practitioner of various forms of martial arts who was "hotter than Bond, cooler than Bullitt."

One day, though, our image of my father as a devoted family man and thriving entrepreneur came crashing down. As we'd come to find out, my father worked hard, but he played a lot harder.

"Someone is having an affair," my mother commented out of the blue.

"What?" Marie commented. We were all sitting around the

dining room table. Marie and I, who were in high school at the time, were finishing homework while Danny colored.

My mother, who was looking out the living room window, casually repeated, "Someone in the neighborhood is having an affair. That Corvette has been parked in the same spot for two weeks."

We all jumped up to see the car my mother was talking about. Surely enough, there was a yellow Corvette parked in front of the vacant lot next door.

"Two weeks? Are you sure?" I asked.

"I'm sure."

"That doesn't mean someone is having an affair," offered Danny, Jr.

"Mmf. I'll bet you," resounded my mother. We all contemplated who it could be. About two weeks later, the doorbell sounded. When I opened the door, there was a tall attractive woman with long, brown hair on our doorstep. She appeared a little uncertain, even nervous.

"Is your mother home?"

"Yes. I'll go get her," I replied. I didn't recognize her and had a feeling that I shouldn't invite her in. I closed the door and ran to get my mom who was downstairs folding laundry.

"Mom, there is a lady at the door for you."

"Who is it?"

"I don't know."

My mother walked upstairs to the front door and opened it.

"Hello. Can I help you?"

"Hi Eleanor. I'm Renee Jenkins."

My mother furrowed her brow. "Yes," she responded quizzically.

The woman hesitated. "I've been having an affair with Daniel. We have a two-year-old daughter. I will help you divorce him."

"What?" My mother stumbled back from the door.

"I know this is a lot to take in. Let me give you my number. Call me." She wrote her name and number on a slip of paper from her pocket and handed it to my mom, and then she was gone. No more yellow Corvette parked in front of the vacant lot. However, she wasn't gone from our lives.

My mother was right. Someone was having an affair—her husband. Our father. This was something none of us ever considered. Our father worked long hours, true, but we idolized him. He wouldn't cheat on our mother! This Renee Jenkins was lying! Why should we believe this stranger, anyway?

My mother, siblings, and I cried in disbelief. My parents had always drilled the Ten Commandments into our heads. Or perhaps that was just my mother. She read the Bible to us every evening before bedtime.

"You shall not commit adultery."

My parents belonged to the First Church of Christ. The church had strict rules as to how its parishioners were to conduct themselves. For the first time in my life, I realized I had no clue who my father was. How could we have been so naïve?

After that encounter, Renee started calling our house, trying to convince our mother to divorce our father.

My mother was adamantly opposed to the idea. First of all, she loved my father. But she also wasn't about to let his girlfriend waltz into their life and upend everything.

"I'm not leaving my husband for you," she told Renee. "I'm not going to leave him so that some tramp can take my place!"

This attitude took Renee by surprise. She'd been expecting the opposite reaction from my mother and had been looking forward to becoming the woman of the house. Unbeknownst to us, my father and Renee had been involved for quite a long time. They'd met at General Electric when he'd worked there briefly after leaving college. After that, he began a cleaning company, and Renee worked there, as well. Of course, my mother hadn't been aware of this relationship all these years.

When my mother ordered Renee to stop calling the house, she started stalking our family. We'd go to the mall and see her there with a child—the child she claimed was our half-sister. One day, I saw a photograph of this child on my father's desk, but I didn't dare ask who she was. Deep down, I knew the truth.

Renee was obsessed with my father and with our family. She seemed to always be in the wings, always around and available. She became close to my father's brothers, so close that my mother claimed that the child could have been fathered by my uncle and not her adulterer husband. Little did we know, Renee's daughter, Tiffany, went on camping and fishing trips with my father, our uncle, and our cousins. When I learned this as an adult, it stung. Why hadn't my father taken us along? How could my family betray us by keeping this affair a secret?

Meanwhile, years passed, and my mother, siblings, and I

believed that Renee was out of the picture. Needless to say, Renee and my father carried on their relationship, and we'd find out in the worst possible way.

Nine years after Renee showed up on our doorstep, our father suffered from a heart attack while they were fooling around in one of his office bedrooms. From what I have heard, the scene went something like this:

"Uhh. My stomach is bothering me," my father rolled over, groaning in pain.

"Do you think you need to use the bathroom?" Renee asked.

"Uhh. God dammit!" my father moaned again from the pain.

"Go to the bathroom, Danny. You'll feel better."

He got up from the bed and stumbled to the bathroom naked. Suddenly, there was a loud thud.

"Danny," Renee called. "What are you doing?" She sighed and got up from the bed they shared.

Renee walked naked across the office, realizing too late the office blinds were open. As she approached the partially open bathroom door, she saw her lover's feet spread across the floor. Running towards him, she pushed open the door and fell to her knees.

"Danny, are you alright?" She shook my father's lifeless body—to no avail. "Oh my God! Oh my God! Danny! Danny!" Renee tried to get him out of the bathtub but couldn't move his heavy body.

"Danny, hang in there. I'll go get help!" She ran to the bedroom and dressed quickly. Jumping into her yellow Corvette, she sped down the street to my Uncle James' house.

"James will know what to do," she thought to herself. Panic-stricken, she drove onto the sidewalk in front of James' home and ran to the front door screaming, "James! James!"

Sharon, James' wife, was watering flowers on the side of the house when she heard Renee's screams. She ran to the front and saw Renee banging hysterically on the door of their small frame home, still screaming James' name.

"Renee? What's going on?" Sharon asked.

James appeared at the door. "What's going on?"

"James…" Renee couldn't speak. As she tried to catch her breath, she began to sob.

"Calm down, Renee! What is it?" James pleaded.

"Daniel fell!" Renee finally got the words out. "He's at the office… in the bathtub. I couldn't move him."

"Did you call 911?" When she didn't respond, James raised his voice, exacerbated. "Renee, did you call 911?"

Renee slowly shook her head, sobbing.

Sharon raced to the phone and called 911 before James could say anything else.

James, unlike Daniel, was a quiet, modest man. He always followed the rules, worked hard, and was kind and respectful to all. He made the 30-minute trip across town in fifteen, running red lights and passing other cars in emergency lanes. When he finally reached the office, he found the exterior door open. In the bathroom, he discovered his older brother naked, having fallen headfirst in the bathtub. Daniel's body was cold to the touch as James tried to lift him from the tub. He heard sirens and was soon surrounded by first responders.

James began to sob. His brother was only 46 years old—and he was dead.

After his death, I was the one who went through my father's belongings. I was 25 at the time and working on my master's. It was amazing to see all that he'd accumulated, and I began to understand the extent of his lavish and secretive lifestyle. He kept two German shepherds inside the office where he died. I'd remembered him saying something about collecting pennies and the best place to hide a diamond, and when I poured out his collection onto the floor, a diamond sat amidst the copper-colored pennies.

My father had been the main employer for his family members. He took care of his siblings, putting tires on their cars and making sure their children were cared for. When he died, they all, in turn, took care of my mother. As you can imagine, her life was completely upended, and my father's siblings came together to get her back on her feet. They helped her sort through her affairs, get an apartment, and receive social security.

My grandparents had also lost their provider. They didn't make enough to care for themselves and their twelve children. When my half-sister appeared at their doorstep, they blamed her for my father's death and slammed the door in her face. Renee and her daughter were strictly prohibited from attending the funeral.

When my father died, my parents had been married over 25 years. Unfortunately, after his death, Renee did not disappear from our lives. In an effort to claim our father's social security check, she brought her case to court and proved that her daughter was our father's child. This resulted in the check being split between Renee and my mother, a terrible outcome for my mother financially. My father hadn't saved any money, so once everything was sold—the house, cars, etc.—there was money for my mother to live off of for a little while, but not very long. By the time I was married, my mother was broke and living off social security.

Renee continued to harbor her unhealthy interest in our family. Later, she took my brother in to live when he came upon hard times. According to her, she always considered my siblings and me as her own children, which I found terribly bizarre. One day, I asked her why she hadn't called 911 after my father had a heart attack. "He was dead," she responded, but I don't believe that.

It wasn't until I was a grown adult that I met my half-sister, Tiffany. She was working at the local credit union, and I said to her, "You look just like my sister." When she told me her name, I was shocked to realize—she was my sister! There continues to be a competition between our mothers, and although my half-sister is somewhat in my life, I don't completely trust her. I see her and her mother as takers, always looking to take advantage of a situation when given the chance.

6

HOUSE ON FIRE

The trauma of abuse is never fully gone.
Its filthy stain never leaves.
It resides in the soul forever

–Author Unknown, n.d.

Perhaps the death of our family began with the death of my father. He had always been the glue, the provider, the overseer. We were accustomed to his forceful hand maintaining total control. Without him, maybe we just didn't know how to be a family anymore.

My father always wanted to have another child, and when I was fourteen years old, his wish was granted. My mother gave birth to my younger sister, Cara, in 1976. By then, my mother's illness had progressed much further along. Cara relied strongly on my father, and his death rocked her world; she was only eleven years old at the time.

My father had always put Cara on a pedestal, never treating her with the violence that the other three of us children had endured. He took Cara golfing and gave her everything she wanted, including all the toys she could dream of and her own bedroom complete with a white furniture set with gold trim.

In the years after my father died, everything spiraled downward. Now that he was gone, Cara was stuck at home with my mother, who was so horribly depressed at times that she wouldn't buy food. Cara would call me crying, but I was away at graduate school. Feeling helpless, I'd call the neighbors to see who could help. Sometimes my Uncle Albert would take Cara in for a few weeks, but my mother always wanted her back. In my mother's mind, there was nothing wrong with the fact that her house was a complete mess, and all she fed her daughter was green peas. In her mind, she was perfectly fine and functional.

My mother repeatedly begged me to move back home to help pay for the house, but the mortgage was well beyond any money I made. I would have had to work two or three jobs, and I simply refused to do that. When Cara was sixteen years old, my mother lost the house.

My mother developed a habit of calling me nonstop, often in the middle of the night. If I didn't wake up in time to pick up the call, she'd leave me a long voicemail full of irrational ranting:

"You tell them freaks I'm not a white confederate. I am not a black confederate. I'm not a stupid confederate. I am no kind of a confederate whatsoever. I do not have a doctor at all. In 1997, I was notified in writing that I was no longer welcome in that system. So, if I'm not welcome, you know darn well I don't

have no white, black, or anything else. Because I don't even have… I can't even go over there. I'm not going to be dumb enough to ask that man if he will take me back when he put it in writing, certified mail that I was not welcome over there. He must be stupid."

It's hard to describe how frightening it was to wake up to her words of insanity. It was like being in a nightmare, except it was the reality of my mother's completely psychotic state of mind. I was working as a mental health clinical director. I could not deal with being awakened again, and again, and again, only to hear her insane rantings and conspiracy theories that only reminded me of how ill my mother was. So sometimes I silenced the ringer on my phone to ensure a night of peaceful sleep, but there was no peace.

Working in the mental health field, I knew that my mother was very ill. It was obvious that she suffered from delusions and hallucinations. Still, it was difficult to withstand the onslaught of emotional abuse from her. Children were not spared her hostility; she didn't act like a grandmother to her grandchildren. When my son Brian was first born, she'd hold him and smile, but as she got older, her behavior shifted. She often made nasty comments about my son, Brian, and barely interacted with Cara's daughter, Maria.

I remember one particularly scary interaction that we had when it became apparent to me that she could harm others. I don't remember the details of the conversation, but I was trying to convince her to get the help that she needed. She became enraged and got a dangerous look in her eyes. She started shaking, and there was a sense that the insanity was taking control over her faculties. I became very frightened and left her apartment, calling her from a nearby phone booth to try to calm her down and offer resources to get help. She refused.

When I played one of my mother's voicemails to my therapist, she affirmed what I'd been feeling; my mother was torturing me. She told me that I needed to cut my mother off. Strangely, it was only then that I realized that I actually had a choice. I didn't need to take this emotional abuse any longer, so I decided to take a break from her for all our sakes.

I cut off contact with my mother for two years… until she made another suicide attempt. I'd always been taught to value my family and take care of them, so I took my mother in after she was released from the hospital. I had a nanny who took care of my young son and my mother. In the beginning, my mother wore diapers and couldn't do basic tasks alone, but over time, she recuperated to a large extent.

Still, having my mother live with us was a nightmare. My husband, son, and I were gone all day between work and day care, and my mother would spend the hours sitting in the sunroom in a thin, inappropriate nightgown where all the neighbors could see her. She ate everything in the fridge and did little else. She would binge for hours at a time on any cookies, cakes, or chips she could find.

I couldn't understand why her bedroom smelled like death until I pulled back the covers one day and saw that the fitted sheet was black; it was horrifying. She'd been pretending to change and wash her sheets.

I had to take time off from work to take her to her psychiatry and therapist appointments. I realized that, instead of taking her medication when I gave it to her, she'd been keeping it or throwing it away in the trash. Eventually, I had to start crushing the meds, putting them in apple sauce, and watching her to make sure she ate it all. The whole experience was exhausting and often embarrassing.

Meanwhile, having my mother live with us was damaging the well-being of my nuclear family. One time, she stood in my kitchen looking at the knives, accusing me of protecting rapists. She looked crazy and delusional. I put the knife rack up high for fear of what she might do with them.

My husband got so angry at the state of her room one day that he threw a lamp against the wall. This type of behavior was completely unlike him, and I was worried that I might lose my husband over this.

She continued to behave aggressively towards my son. One time, she fell and bruised the entire side of her body. When she blamed Brian for the fall, accusing him of pushing her, it was the last straw. Even while taking her medication, she was toxic, and we couldn't have her staying with us any longer. Although it went against everything that I believed about family values, I moved my mother into an assisted living facility.

7

MARIE: FROM CLOSEST CONFIDANT TO STRANGER, AND BACK AGAIN

"Alone in grief, alone in thought she stood…"

–Cefai, n.d.

Mornings in our household were nightmarish. I remember trying desperately to hide behind my older sister, Marie. Born only eleven months apart, we were Irish twins and desperately close as children. My survival approach was to be invisible; perhaps if my parents couldn't see me, they'd leave me alone. Sometimes, it seemed to work, and I was spared their ridicule and disapproval. Other mornings, I wasn't so fortunate.

"God you're so ugly!" my mother shouted on one such morning, as she yanked the comb through my unruly hair.

In my tri-racial family, everyone looked different. I was the only one with kinky hair. By contrast, Marie's loose curls were silky and smooth, and my mother's hair was so long and beautiful that white people would stroke it admiringly. Unlike me, Marie didn't look black. None of my siblings did. In the summer, my skin would turn jet black, and my hair reddened. Being dark in my family wasn't seen as a good thing.

"Marie looks just like you, Daniel!" my mother said to our father, who had sandy-colored hair and light features. They both stared adoringly at their eldest daughter, commenting on her rosy cheeks, cherub face, and silky black curls. Marie looked vaguely Middle Eastern. Bending down, my mother kissed Marie softly on the cheek. "My little apple dumpling!" she cooed.

"I think Danny looks like you as well," she said to my father, petting my little brother's head. "I'm not sure who Karen looks like." That's how I was treated in my family: as an afterthought, an ugly outsider.

Still, Marie was my protector. I knew that if I stayed close to her, I was safe, because nothing was going to happen to Marie, the family favorite. I felt more attached to my sister than I did to my own mother. But she was too young to be a protector. It was a heavy role for someone so young. I was like Marie's shadow, and at times, she hid from me to be free from my constant presence.

In high school, we were best friends—attached at the hip. We did all the same extracurricular activities, like cheerleading and track. When you saw one of us, the other was never far. That's how we ended up attending the same college. But even as teenagers, Marie and I received very different treatment from our parents.

My mother wanted someone to help her take care of our baby sister, Cara; more often than not, my mother asked me to make the sacrifice instead of Marie, who remained my mother's favorite child.

Later, as an adult, my mother would make comments like, "Karen, I know you felt like your father loved Maria more than you." In response, I'd say, "No, Mom. I never told you that. You're the one saying that."

When it was time for Marie to go to college, my father made a big deal of the affair, buying her a brand-new set of luggage and driving her to campus. On the other hand, when it was my turn to go to college a year later, my father asked me to stay home to help my mother. Although he made a significant amount of money, he wouldn't pay for me to attend college, so I was forced to sit out a year to be able to qualify for financial aid. When it came time to go to campus, a friend of mine drove me because I was afraid to drive on the highway. In my father's mind, I wasn't meant to go to college.

When I first got to college, Marie and I were together, but after my first year, Marie got pregnant and dropped out. Like with my mother, it seems like the rapidly changing hormones during pregnancy make the women in my family crazy—and with every kid, they seem to get crazier. Around this time, Marie became hyper religious and started treating me very strangely, accusing me of being too wild and a sinner. Every time I would call her, she would say hateful, nasty, and cold-hearted things to me. Eventually, we stopped talking altogether, which made me terribly sad considering how close we'd been all my life.

Marie's first husband, Peter, was attractive, smart, and an overall good guy. She wanted to live out our mother's dream. Still, she felt like he was beneath her.

I watched from afar as my sister's behavior went from strange to insane. When her children were very small, she became obsessed with a military officer living next door. Even though they were both married, she blatantly flirted with him and sent him roses. The military officer had to tell Peter to please get a hold of his wife.

Later, Marie moved to New Mexico to get a bachelor's degree. She did well, but things started to go south when she went for her master's. She ended up dropping out of the program, because she was convinced that her department chair was out to get her. It was during these times when she felt others were out to get her that she'd reach out to me. I'd listen as she ranted about the latest injustice she'd endured, never quite knowing how much to believe. Eventually, though, her paranoia would shift back towards me, and I'd become the villain again.

One morning, I received a strange call from Peter. "Karen," he said, his voice trembling. "Marie wants to kill me."

At the time, I thought he was joking. Peter was always telling bad jokes. "What do you mean she wants to kill you?"

"She wants to kill me," he reiterated. "And, I think she was going to."

I listened as Peter explained how Marie had pulled out a large butcher knife from beneath their mattress early in the morning. His voice shook as he described seeing the knife in her hand.

"She said that I was kidnapping and killing children in our

neighborhood here in Oklahoma!" Peter said. "And she accused me of killing children when we were stationed in Germany. She said that I chopped the children's bodies up and hid them!" He sounded thoroughly distressed. "You know me. I would never do that! How could she even say that?"

At the time, Marie and I had grown distant. This was not my choice. She'd refused to talk to me for several years. At the time, I didn't understand that Marie's actions were driven by her growing paranoia.

"She's struggling with depression," Peter said. "She didn't want anyone to know, but she just admitted herself to James River Psychiatric."

The day after I spoke to Peter, Marie called me. "Karen, I need you to come to Oklahoma, but you'll need to stay with a friend of mine—not with Peter and the kids. I don't trust Peter."

"Where are you, Marie?" I asked.

"I'm at a hospital. I admitted myself after I kept having problems with my car and Peter. Peter is hurting children in the neighborhood."

"Marie, what makes you say that?"

"I heard him talking about it."

"You heard him say what and to whom?"

"I don't know who he was talking to, but he was telling them where he hid the children's bodies. He cut their bodies up into small pieces so that they couldn't be found."

I didn't know how to respond to her outlandish claims.

"I need you to come here," she continued. "Will you come?"

I agreed to stay with her friend, a stranger to me, even though my brother-in-law, niece, and nephew were nearby. I talked to Marie's friend later that day. She seemed very nice and expressed concern for Marie's well-being.

I didn't want to go to Oklahoma alone, but Stephen had to work. It was bad enough that I was taking off from work; we really couldn't afford it. I flew to Oklahoma the next morning, filled with dread.

When I arrived at James River Psychiatric, I was surprised by how pleasant the facility looked. It wasn't scary at all.

Marie had told me several times that her car was being vandalized, so when I arrived, I found her Jeep in the parking lot to check it out. After a thorough examination, though, I couldn't find any scratches on the car.

Peter was already at the hospital and had arranged for us to meet with Marie's psychiatrist. Dr. Smith told us that Marie had schizoaffective disorder, bipolar type, and described the symptoms of her illness and prognosis. Peter answered Dr. Smith's questions regarding the history of Marie's illness, which had up to this point been symptoms of depression. Dr. Smith told us that he was quite sure of Marie's diagnosis. Like my mother, people with this disorder could easily hide their illness and refuse treatment.

When I went to Marie's room to see her, she seemed totally normal, but she made it clear that she didn't want to see her husband, Peter. Marie was having trouble filling out a questionnaire, and I was trying to help her, when she stopped abruptly.

"Did you see that?" she asked.

"See what?" I said.

"Shadows. I keep seeing shadows falling along the wall."

I looked at the wall and shook my head. I wasn't seeing whatever it was she was seeing. Later, she brought up something very strange and surprising from our childhood.

"I remember having sex with dad," she said matter-of-factly. "You were in the room."

"No, Marie. I don't remember anything like that happening. That never happened when I was around, and you and I were usually together."

"I guess you're right," Marie replied.

After Marie was discharged from the psychiatric facility, Peter and her children were terrified to have her back at home, unsure of what she was capable of. They locked themselves in their bedrooms at night while Marie slept on the living room couch. She had become a stranger in her own home.

Marie and Peter got divorced shortly after this episode, and she asked me if she could come and live with me and my family in Virginia. To be honest, I was scared of her, too. Knowing her competitive streak, I worried about how she would behave around my husband. Eventually, she went back to Roanoke and stayed with our mother, who was suffering from her version of the same disease.

In 1997, my family and I had moved back to Central Virginia, which is very rural. I have always preferred more urban areas for their diversity and opportunities. As the illnesses played out in my family members' lives, I felt the locals in Central Virginia were judging us. There were people around us who had never ventured outside of the city limits, or even made the trip to Roanoke, Virginia—only 30 minutes away.

At that time, I worked for a local mental health agency, providing therapy services to individuals suffering from illnesses much like my family's. I have always enjoyed helping others. Unknowingly, I believe a part of me also wanted to get closer to home, to reconnect, and find out more about the illness that overwhelmed my family.

One day, I came home for lunch break, rushing as usual. I let the dogs out and checked my voicemails. There was a message from Stephen.

"Sweetie, Les just called. He said Marie had a heart attack. I'm getting ready to go into session, but call me, and I'll try to pick up."

Les was Marie's second husband. In shock, I tried to reach Stephen. When he didn't pick up, I dialed Les, who also didn't pick up. Then, I called my mother to see if she knew anything.

"There is nothing wrong with Marie," my mother retorted. "As usual, you're overreacting."

I hung up the phone, feeling like I was in The Twilight Zone. I was worried about Marie, but I also felt that Les would have notified my mother if there was something wrong. I called Cara, my youngest sister, whose reaction was like my mother's.

"I've got to get back to work," Cara replied bluntly, with no apparent concern for our oldest sister.

Again, my mother and sister were locked in their own realities, not able to consider any information to the contrary, not even when faced with stark realities. I felt alone. As a teen, I was able to turn to my sister and even my mother at times. We could discuss anything, but now they were closed off—locked away inside their own minds. My mother and sisters were living but gone. I kept trying to get them back, but that would never happen. Living near them made it all more painful.

My sisters were both very lovely, sweet, demure, kind, and smart—but like Jekyll and Hyde, they could also switch on a dime and become crazy, mean, and hateful.

Eventually, I got Les on the phone.

"She had a heart attack taking those kids to Kentucky. I told her not to go, but you know how Marie is." At the time, Marie was working on a master's in curriculum and instruction. I remembered her having said something about going on a trip to take her students to a competition.

"She's at Kentucky State Hospital," Les continued. "I'm on my way there now." He sounded tired. He was quite a bit older than Marie—seventeen years older.

I called the hospital in Kentucky, and the nurse on duty said that Marie was stable, but I had a bad feeling. I drove to the airport and boarded a plane for Kentucky. I wished Stephen could come with me, but he had to work and take care of Brian, our son, who was five years old at the time.

Meanwhile, Danny was driving from Roanoke; he arrived in Kentucky at the same time as I did. I never rode with Danny anywhere. He drove like my father—fast and reckless. Over the years, he'd had his fair share of speeding tickets and had even lost his license over reckless driving a couple of times.

At the hospital, Danny and I nearly ran to the elevator, taking it to the fourth floor. The hallway was a maze of units, but we finally made it to Marie's room at the end of a hallway. Les was sitting in a chair beside her bed.

Marie looked very pale in a blue and white hospital gown beneath white bed sheets. She was intubated and her breathing was ragged, the only sign we had that she was still alive.

Marie had always been thin; like our mother, she weighed under a hundred pounds after three kids. But as she got sicker, her bad habits caught up to her. She was always in a hurry, snacking on sugary foods and slurping on a "Big Gulp" or Mountain Dew. Perhaps binge eating was another form of addiction for Marie, same as it was for our mother, who had been known to eat an entire cake when she lived with me and Stephen. Marie always talked about losing weight, but by the time she was lying in the hospital, she weighed 215 pounds—a lot of weight for her small 5'3" frame to carry.

The doctor came in to check on Marie. He told us that she had had a stroke.

"It's not normal for a 38-year-old woman to have a stroke. We're running tests to determine what's going on."

"I thought she had a heart attack," Danny muttered.

"She had a stroke on the right side of her brain," the doctor stated. He provided a cautious prognosis for Marie's recovery.

"I need a smoke!" Danny replied and walked briskly out of the room.

I sat in a chair and just watched Marie. I didn't want to take my eyes off my sister for fear that she would die. Danny, Les, and I stayed with Marie that night.

The next day, Marie gained consciousness. I had fallen asleep in the chair but woke up to Marie mumbling, "Get the bag to the plane. Get the bag to the plane." Marie continued to mumble the same words for most of the day. She seemed frustrated that she couldn't communicate with us. At times, she was tearful. During other moments, she appeared to give up, exasperated and worn from her failed attempts.

Marie was paralyzed on the left side of her body. I tried to calm her by giving her ice chips, putting a cool towel on her head, and brushing her hair.

I called my mother to let her know how Marie was doing. "Marie is fine," was all she could say.

Next, I phoned Cara. "Cara, are you coming to Kentucky?"

"No. I'm sure Marie is going to be fine."

"Well, at least talk to her. She's right beside me…" At that point, Marie reached for the phone.

"Where are you?" Marie said audibly, despite her paralysis. Marie handed the phone back to me, exhausted from the sheer effort.

"I'm on my way," Cara stated flatly.

Cara arrived at the hospital the next morning. She had a surprise for us: she was newly married.

"Hey!" Cara walked into Marie's Kentucky hospital room with her new husband, Michael. She was in her own world. Perhaps it was being a newlywed. Perhaps her flippant mood was foreshadowing her own illness to come. Whatever the cause, neither Cara nor my mother ever seemed to truly acknowledge the gravity of Marie's illness.

Meanwhile, Les was being instructed by the occupational therapist on how to feed Marie to ensure that she didn't aspirate.

"You have to make sure that none of the food is pocketed or collected in her mouth without being chewed, because this can cause her to choke," the OT said. She couldn't easily clear the left side of her mouth because of the paralysis on the left side.

Les looked uncomfortable, like he wanted to be rescued from the task of feeding his partially paralyzed wife. I felt sick as I watched.

Then Peter, her first husband, showed up with their two kids. He really did love Marie but felt he had no choice but to divorce her after she had threatened him so harshly and accused him of such horrid atrocities. It was awkward having two men who loved Marie in the same hospital room.

In recent years, Marie had developed Antiphospholipid Antibody Syndrome, which meant her blood was prone to clotting. She had to stay on blood thinners, but we soon found out that the doctors hadn't been giving her any during her hospitalization.

A few days later, Marie was transferred to a Roanoke hospital for care so that she could be near her young son. I took the opportunity to visit my own son and get all the things that my sister had requested me to bring—special foods and magazines. I was exhausted from the long days at the hospital and grateful to spend a night in my own bed.

In the morning, I got a call from the hospital to come right away. The moment I pushed open the door to her hospital room,

I caught the doctors with paddles on my sister's body, a trail of red liquid dribbling from her mouth. Her body was raised in a way that looked completely unnatural.

"You're not supposed to be here," a doctor said, but I ran into the room anyway. I watched in horror as the doctors tried to save my sister but simply couldn't.

My oldest sister was gone. I felt completely empty, like I should be dead, because I had never been alive without her.

I called my mother to give her the news. Going to her apartment was out of the question. My mother had stopped her medication and was psychotic.

"Mom, Marie didn't make it. She passed away a few minutes ago."

"Sure, Karen," my mother replied in a sarcastic voice. She had never come to the hospital to see her oldest daughter. She hadn't been able to say goodbye to Marie.

Later, my mother wouldn't, or couldn't, acknowledge Marie's death.

Once, after my mother was stabilized on medication again, Stephen and I went to visit my mother at her apartment. She greeted us pleasantly at the door and then said, "Did you hear Karen died?"

I was shocked at first, but then my shock turned to anger. I was outraged and hurt that my mother had refused to accept the truth about Marie's death and would rather that I be the one that had passed away.

In the weeks before Marie died, a strange thing happened: Marie started treating me like the sister from our childhood. Something changed in her, and it was as if nothing had ever happened between us. All of her hate and rage from the last twenty years disappeared, and we were as close as ever.

I know my sister loved me, and I recognize now that her illness got in the way of our relationship. I'm grateful that, at least for a little while, my sister and I were able to be loving and kind to each other. I'll hold on to that memory forever.

8

MOMMY ISSUES

One morning in 1999, a man called my house.

"Mrs. Kaiser," he said, "this is Howard Justis from Raintree Apartments. I'm calling because I'm quite concerned about your mother."

"What's happening? What's wrong?" I remembered the familiar feeling of fear and foreboding, knowing very well how bizarre my mother's behavior could be.

"Well," he said, "some of the residents told me that Eleanor was yelling out of her window as they walked by. I went to check on her, and she accused me of stealing her menstrual period through the microwave. She said she knew what I was up to."

"She's very ill," I said. "I think she stopped taking her medication."

"I'm quite concerned. Some of our residents are very elderly and fragile. I believe she could hurt one of them. Can you come talk to her?"

"Mr. Justis, I'm afraid that won't do any good. I've tried to reason with her when she's been like this in the past. It never works. She just gets more agitated. The police need to be called. She's going to need an emergency custody order to be hospitalized."

"Well, can you do that? I don't like getting involved in these matters."

"Alright. I'll try. I'll be there in a few minutes."

I didn't know how to help my mother back then. I was afraid, embarrassed, and out of answers. The situation made me feel very alone and burdened. There is no manual for these life circumstances.

In the end, my mother was admitted to North Eastern State Hospital, a state psychiatric facility, and hospitalized for several months. It was her fourth state hospital admission, and she'd be hospitalized at least twice more afterwards.

When she was discharged, she was just as delusional as when she was admitted. I'll never forget the conversation I had with her attending psychiatrist.

"I believe in compromising with the patient. And, if I clear your mother of the psychosis completely, she will have huge holes in her memory."

I remember slamming down the phone; this doctor was more than just a little arrogant and cocky! I can't share the disparaging words I used to describe him afterwards.

The doctor didn't believe that my mother was dangerous. His logic for doing nothing about her psychosis was that ridding her of it would also rid her of her recent memory; in essence, when psychotic patients are stable, they don't remember what they did when their mood was extreme.

But it was my belief that to do nothing was much more dangerous. She needed to be on a medication like Risperdal, but instead my mother was prescribed even less medication than before the hospitalization.

The most important thing to do in these cases is eliminate the psychosis so it doesn't develop further. These illnesses are progressive, and the longer a patient is psychotic, the more damage is done to the brain. My mother was losing more gray matter with every psychotic episode. What the doctor was doing was ruining my mother's life and signing her death sentence.

9

UNRAVELING: DANNY'S DOWNWARD SPIRAL

I woke to the sound of a baby crying. Or at least, I thought I heard a baby crying. It must have been a dream.

Suddenly, I was fully awake, remembering the events from the last two days. Tears began rolling down my face. My brother, Danny, was gone.

Danny was a lot like my father; he could fix anything. But, like my father, he could be volatile and explosive. He was prone to angry outbursts and often chain smoked out of anxiety. He dropped out of high school and got his GED. When he was fifteen, he made his first suicide attempt by swallowing a bottle of Tylenol. After that, he was hospitalized, but my parents refused to get him the counseling that he needed. Then he joined the military, where he attempted suicide for the second time. He was hospitalized but not discharged from the military. Eventually, he went AWOL and was court marshalled, leading to a dishonorable discharge.

He married Stephanie when she was only sixteen; she was also a high school dropout and worked in factories for a paycheck. Eventually, they had two children together, little Danny and Laura. Unfortunately, those children were often neglected by their parents. I remember one particularly bad story about Laura when she was only two years old. My brother, Danny, was supposed to be watching her while his wife worked long shifts, but he forgot about his little girl and left her sitting on the bed all night while he was out doing who knows what. She must have been starving and extremely uncomfortable in a dirty diaper.

I didn't see too much of my brother over the years except for holidays and when he came around to ask for money. He was reclusive and distrustful; he didn't like me speaking to his wife when he wasn't around. Over time, he became more aggressive. When our sister, Cara, was pregnant with her daughter, Maria, Danny threw a large rock at her, barely missing. Then there was the story about the time he hit Stephanie with the car, and another time when he threw a 37-inch color TV at his teenage son. I didn't want to be around someone like that, someone who reminded me so much of my father.

Stephanie was the glue that held Danny together—for better or for worse. She grew up with an alcoholic father, and, having developed codependent tendencies from a young age, she was always trying to fix Danny. Over time, it became too much for Stephanie to handle—Danny's cheating, drinking, and violent outbursts. At first, Stephanie just had an occasional glass of wine after the children went to bed. Soon, one glass turned into two… then three… until she was drinking every single day to the point of numbness. She'd always been the stable one, but now she was drowning her sorrows in alcohol.

Eventually, after 22 years of marriage, Stephanie left him. Danny, desperate to find another rock to prop him up and enable him, hastily met and married Lynn.

Lynn seemed highly manipulative and even more unstable than my brother. She was a Klonopin-addicted alcoholic who appeared to have a mood disorder and borderline personality disorder. Lynn accused my brother of breaking her ribs and puncturing her lung, but Danny believed it was Lynn's stepfather who was beating her up—and that the two of them were sleeping together.

Danny started to follow Lynn around town dressed in his old Army fatigues with his face painted black as if he were going into combat. He followed her to work and kept logs of Lynn's activity, trying to catch her cheating on him. Late at night, he'd show up at our uncle's house dressed like that. It was more than bizarre. This was Roanoke, Virginia—not a warzone!

My brother's psychosis seemed to express itself differently than it did with my mother and sisters. He exhibited signs of extreme paranoia but showed no evidence of hallucinations. Often, at least for me, it was hard to get a handle on whether what he was saying was true or completely irrational.

Lynn obtained a restraining order against Danny, but within days, she violated the restraining order by going to his house. She said that she wanted to work things out and that she was going to drop the restraining order. Lynn asked my sister, Cara, if she would babysit her son from a previous relationship, Matthew, while she and Danny went on dates. Cara agreed.

Later, when Danny arrived at their scheduled court date, he expected Lynn to drop the restraining order as promised. Instead, Lynn showed up to court with her stepfather and told the judge that she didn't want to drop the restraining order. She told the judge that Danny had contacted her, and this violated the restraining order.

Danny phoned me after court that morning to recount what had happened.

"She tricked me, Karen," he said, sounding desolate. "Why would she do that?"

"I'm not sure, Danny. But what did the judge say?"

Danny never was able to give me a coherent explanation of the judge's order, but it was clear that he expected to be picked up by the police. He was also convinced that the Commonwealth's attorney's office was considering upgrading the charges to malicious wounding, which carried a mandatory one-to-five years in prison.

"I'm not going to jail, Karen," he said.

"I'm so sorry, Danny."

It seemed unreal that Danny could have gotten into so much trouble. He had only been married to Lynn for a few months, and he was already facing a prison sentence? But, was any of this true…? I couldn't tell what the truth was anymore—what was reality? What was delusion? What mattered most was that it was true to Danny. And he was distraught, believing that he had been betrayed by his wife and that he would be incarcerated.

Later that day, I called Danny back to see how he was doing. Every time I talked to him, he sounded more troubled and lost.

"Danny, how are you? Where are you?"

"I'm home," he said, slurring his words. Later, I'd find out that he'd run his truck into a tree and totaled it that night.

"What are you doing?"

"I picked up a six pack of beer and a box of Kraft Kreme donuts." He paused, then spoke again. "Karen, do you know what a gun sounds like when it is fired?"

I stammered, confused. "N-n-no."

I heard a loud "CRACK."

Panicked, I tried to think of what I could say to calm him down. "Danny, what do you think about coming to stay with me for a while—until you feel better?"

"I'm all good."

"Danny, are you planning to shoot yourself?"

"Yep. After I eat my doughnuts and drink a beer…" He sounded as if he were high on something. "Lynn won," he continued. "I'm going to jail."

"Danny, what about the family? What about Laura and little Danny? Please don't do this."

"I don't care about little Danny or Laura. All I want is Lynn." A few seconds later, he hung up.

I called 911 and told the dispatcher that my brother had a gun and was planning to shoot himself. The whole thing seemed surreal. I had a horrible feeling that my brother was going to die, but there didn't seem to be anything that I could do to stop it. I was losing him, or perhaps I'd lost him a long time ago…

I tried repeatedly to reach Danny, to no avail. I called the

Roanoke police again to see if they could tell me anything. The officer who answered hesitated and put me on hold. He came back to the phone and told me someone would be calling me back.

A police officer phoned me about ten minutes later. Feeling the desperation mounting inside me, I asked him if my brother was alive.

"No ma'am," he said.

I dropped the phone and began screaming. I couldn't stop screaming.

Stephen, my husband, called my Uncle James, who went to identify my brother's body at the police's request. The next morning, Stephen and I drove to Roanoke. I wanted to go to my brother's home and see for myself where he had died. My Uncle James tried to prepare me for what I was about to see: an open box of Kraft Kreme doughnuts covered in blood, a solitary beer sitting on a small table, and a six pack on the floor. Danny's body had been removed earlier. I would never see my brother again.

My brother had shot himself in the head. He was only 42 years old.

Since, his children have both graduated from high school, but there are lingering effects of the trauma they endured. His son has a tic but won't see a doctor about it. His teeth are rotten, but he won't get them fixed. It's something if he combs his hair. His daughter is emotionally labile, drinks to excess, and dates abusive men. Neither could finish college. They both continue to wear the scars from abuse and neglect, refusing to get help—refusing to get the therapy they so desperately need, much like Danny. They blame Lynn, their father's ex-wife, for their father's death. I've never heard them say a disparaging word about their father. I imagine that, like me, they have mixed feelings regarding their parents—a mix of love and hate, possibly adoration and disgust.

I've never told them about that last conversation that I had with their father. He was so ill at that point; he didn't care about anyone—not even his children. He'd been sick for a long time already; unfortunately, like so many of my family members, he wasn't able, or simply refused, to get the help that he needed to heal.

10

CARA: FROM BABY SISTER TO TRAIN WRECK

One other person remains from my immediate family—Cara. But she hasn't had it easy. When she was eighteen, she moved in with my family and lived with us for a few years while she attended George Mason University. Eventually, though, she dropped out because she was so depressed. I think living alone with my mother after my father died and the rest of us had moved out of the house was toxic for Cara and perhaps led to many of the issues that she had later in life.

After dropping out of college, Cara decided to join the military. She did well and was honorably discharged five years later. Around that time, she became pregnant with her daughter, Maria. Again, like my mother and older sister Marie, pregnancy affected Cara psychologically, and she became very ill. When Maria was young, Cara got into the habit of giving her daughter away to others to take care, because she wasn't able to function normally. She became paranoid and stopped speaking to me, worried that I would steal her child. Ironically, many years later, I would be given custody of

Maria when Cara was deemed unfit as a mother.

Anytime Cara became manic, she got into her car and drove. She'd drive long distances without a plan. For example, one time she drove all the way to Utah to join the Mormon Church. Another time, she went to Alabama and had a terrible accident. The department of social services called me to pick up Maria, so I did. I brought her back to Virginia, but I was afraid to have her in my care, because I wasn't sure what Cara was capable of. So, I called my brother and my aunt so they could care for Maria between the two of them. Meanwhile, Cara had recovered from the accident and was medically cleared but still in the psychiatric hospital.

When Cara was released and came to pick up Maria, my aunt recounted to me how scary she looked. I've experienced it myself. Cara can go from childlike to spitting mad within seconds; it's as if she has multiple personalities. When she gets angry and starts cursing, she can sound like a wild animal. It's frightening.

Cara also developed delusions about Maria's father, whom she had only dated for two weeks. One time, she believed that he had told her to drive them to Atlanta, Georgia, so she did. And then there they were, Cara and little Maria, standing outside of a city building at dusk while the city was becoming vacated. Cara began to cry, and a man and his wife came up and asked if she was OK. She told them that her husband hadn't shown up, so the strangers brought her into their home and let Cara and Maria spend the night. The couple called me and explained the situation. Then they put her on a bus and sent her back home.

Cara's delusions often appear to evolve in ways that help her defend against pain. Now that I have custody of Maria, Cara believes that Maria's biological father owns my house in Lake Manassas so that Maria can have a nice place to live.

At first glance, Cara's thoughts and behavior appear impulsive and erratic. But upon closer inspection, there is always a great deal of thought on Cara's part, even obsessive thought, that precedes her beliefs and ultimate behavior.

Over the years, Cara has been known to disappear without a trace. One time when I couldn't get a hold of her, I tracked her down and found that she and Maria—who was only two years old at the time—were living on the sidewalk in a Walmart parking lot. I tried to get her to go to the hospital, but she wouldn't because she knew she couldn't take Maria with her.

Another time, in 2017, I searched Cara's name on the Internet after having not heard from her for quite a while. Honestly, I was worried that maybe she'd died unexpectedly. Instead, I discovered that my sister was incarcerated in Mississippi after failing to follow the instructions of a police officer. It turns out she was defecating in the middle of a Walmart parking lot. Rather than listen to the police officer, she got into a scuffle with him.

At some point, Cara went to live in Virginia Beach with her friend Joy. Not long after, Joy phoned us when Cara started to act bizarre. According to Joy, Cara was searching the trailer for matches or a lighter with the intention to set herself and Maria on fire. When she couldn't find either in the trailer, she attempted to leave the trailer to look for them. Thankfully, Joy had hidden her car keys so that she couldn't leave.

I asked Joy if she could call 911 to get Cara help, but she said that she couldn't do it and asked if I could talk to Cara. I told her it wouldn't do any good; she needed to be hospitalized.

I knew that Cara is, and was, dangerous. She has been for years. The family had tried to get help for her and Maria, her small child. In the process, we had been transformed into the bad guys. We ended up getting secondary trauma from judges, therapists, police officers, and hospital staff. We were often blamed for not doing enough, for doing too much…

I decided to call 911 myself, not realizing that I would only be able to report local emergencies; the dispatch gave me the phone number to the Virginia Beach police.

I explained to the officer what was happening—that my sister has schizophrenia and that she was trying to set herself and her daughter on fire. I provided the address to Joy's trailer and asked if the police officer would call me to tell me how Cara and Maria were doing. It was hard knowing that loved ones are in danger hours away and there is little you can do to protect them without placing yourself in harm's way.

The police officer said they would check it out. I waited for them to call back, feeling sick to my stomach. I was also angry that Joy hadn't called, herself. I understood not wanting to get involved and not wanting to upset Cara. But Joy knew just as well as I did that Cara wasn't well. Joy's solution was to follow Cara around the trailer, trying to keep her from leaving and hiding Cara's car keys, matches, and lighters. At some point, Joy would need to go to work. What then?

The phone rang, and it was the police officer calling back.

"Ms. Kaiser, your sister and her daughter are fine."

"You spoke to my sister, and everything is OK?"

"Yes, ma'am. Her roommate answered the door. We asked to speak to your sister. She answered our questions. Her daughter was playing nearby. Everything is fine."

"Thank you, Officer." I didn't know what else to say or do. Like so many times before, my efforts to help seemed ineffective and futile. However, the next morning, I received a phone call from my Aunt Theresa, who lived nearby.

"Karen, can you come get Maria?"

"Why? What's going on?"

"I just got a phone call from Frances. She works for Child Protective Services now. The police just took Cara into custody, and Frances has Maria."

"How did CPS get Maria?"

"Frances was at Cara's when she was detained. She told the police that Maria's aunt lives nearby and arranged to bring Maria here, to us. Can you come get her?"

"I have to go to work, but I'll see if Danny can pick Maria up and bring her here. Hopefully, he can stay with her until I get off work." I called Danny hoping he was in a good mood. I never knew what state of mind he was going to be in.

"Danny, Cara was just detained, and Maria is with Aunt Theresa. Can you bring her to our house and stay with her until I get off work?"

"Karen, what did you do?"

I sighed. "Danny, I'm not sure why Cara was detained. I called the police last night to check on Maria after Joy called me to say that Cara was trying to set them both on fire so that they could 'Go be with Jesus.' The police conducted a welfare check and told me that both were fine. I don't know what happened since last night except Maria needs someone to take care of her. Aunt Theresa has to work. Can you help?"

"Sure. I'll go get her right now."

We found out later, after Child Protective Services went to the trailer and removed Maria, that Joy was a hoarder. She had junk stacked from the floor to the ceiling of her trailer with only a small path from the door to the kitchen. The only way to get around was by crawling over furniture, bags of garbage, books, toys, and boxes.

I was grateful for Danny stepping in to help, but I also felt like I had been hit by a truck. "Will this ever end?" I thought. Again, I recalled events of the past, those involving another unwell family member of mine: my mother.

Like my mom in 1999, Cara was hospitalized for six months at a state psychiatric hospital after the incident in Joy's trailer. Once she was discharged from the hospital, we invited her to live with us. She and Maria stayed with us for four years. We fostered both Cara and Maria. Cara parented Maria. Stephen and I were the back-up. This took a great toll on our marriage.

My mother was already living with us. Stephen and I could barely take the conflict caused by my mother's behavior, and now we had Cara and Maria living with us to top it all off. During all this, our own child became ill. We took him to doctor after doctor but couldn't get a diagnosis for many years. Eventually, we found out that Brian had severe obstructive sleep apnea. He had several procedures, but the final surgery could not be performed until he was eighteen. We were exhausted and in a constant state of grief. Stephen had taken all that he could, and frankly, so had I.

Eventually, my mother moved out, first to a nearby assisted living facility. Cara and Maria moved out soon after. I helped Cara find an apartment, co-signed, and had the utilities put in my name. Cara had bad credit from countless hospitalizations, moves, and unpaid bills.

Stephen and I had some semblance of peace for five years. For five years, Cara was able to care for herself and Maria. She had help from family and neighbors; they managed. That was eight years ago.

But the peace didn't last. Late one evening in April of 2011, I received a phone call from Maria, who was eleven years old at the time.

"Aunt Karen," Maria was sobbing.

"What's going on?" I said, instantly fully awake.

"Mom told me to leave."

As it turned out, Cara told Maria that she had to leave, because she was going to go be with Jesus. Maria left their apartment and tried to find a neighbor to stay with, but no one was home. Fortunately, Maria had a cell phone to call me. I called around to find someone to pick her up, and a cousin was available.

The next day, we drove to my cousin's home and picked up Maria. That was April 8, 2011. Stephen and I took Cara to court for custody of Maria. We were in court for two years until we were finally granted full custody. Next, I attempted to obtain child support from Cara's father, who fought it every step of the way. I battled in court for over a year before he was court ordered to pay us child support of $800 a month when Maria was fourteen years old.

In 2018, after a couple of months of no word from Cara, I searched her name on the Internet. Once again, I feared she was dead. I was horrified to find out that she had punched a firefighter, and worse, the house next door to her had burned to the ground, killing one person. According to the official report, the punch was unprovoked, and Cara had yelled at the firefighter, "What are you doing here, b***?"

"Stephen…" I could barely speak. Stephen was sleeping soundly next to me.

"What? What?" he mumbled, quickly stirring. The events of the past 27 years left Stephen and I in a state of hypervigilance, always ready to react to the next imminent emergency.

"Cara has been arrested for punching a firefighter!"

"You're kidding."

"I wish I were."

I turned the laptop so that Stephen could read what I had just read, still in shock. Stephen quickly read the article aloud.

"Do you think she set the fire?" I asked, thinking about the time she had attempted to set herself and her daughter, Maria, on fire.

Stephen, fully awake now, responded softly, "I don't know."

Sitting up in bed, he and I stared at the computer screen, Cara's mugshot staring back at us, her eyes glazed, her face worn with fatigue. We knew her expression and her appearance all too well. We could see the illness in her face and prayed that whoever was caring for her could see the illness, too. Like so many nights before, sleep did not come quickly that night.

The next day, I searched the Virginia Judicial System case status records online hoping to find some information on Cara. As it turns out, Cara was charged with a class 6 felony for assaulting the firefighter. Next, I phoned the Jefferson County jail.

"Hi. My name is Karen Kaiser, and my sister is Cara Williams. She punched a firefighter last month."

"Just a moment while I transfer you to medical."

I was shocked. I couldn't believe in the age of HIPAA, someone might answer my questions, and we would be able to find Cara.

I wondered why they were transferring me to medical. It makes sense, I thought to myself. Schizophrenia, diabetes, high blood pressure… she definitely should be in medical. However, I was surprised. In my experience, jails were not the best at providing medical care. Cara must be in really bad shape, I thought quietly.

A nurse came onto the phone. "Medical," she said.

"Hi. My name is Karen Kaiser. I'm trying to find my sister, Cara Williams. She punched a firefighter last month."

"Yes. She's here."

"Is she alright?"

"Yes, ma'am."

"I'm not sure if you know, but Cara has diabetes, high blood pressure, and schizoaffective disorder, bipolar type. She is disabled and receives services from the Jefferson County Veteran's Administration." The nurse seemed to be taking down the information that I provided, asking me to repeat the diagnosis of schizoaffective disorder.

"Can she have visitors?" I asked.

"You have to be on the visitor's list," she responded. "I'll let her know that you called."

"Thank you."

I began reflecting back on the events of the past twenty plus years—my mother, older sister, Danny, and Cara, all affected by varying degrees of the same illness.

Cara has been incarcerated or hospitalized over a year. To this day, Cara denies the fact that there was even a fire. However, the home burned to the ground, and somebody died. The firefighter that Cara punched probably saved her life! She could have walked into a burning home.

We try desperately to communicate with Cara but run into one obstacle after another. She is not that far away in miles, but the traffic between Northern Virginia and Jefferson County puts us hours apart. She bounces between the state hospital and the jail, as the judicial system tries to settle on a verdict that is fitting for her immensely complicated situation. Cara's chronic mental illness, her dissociative episodes, her violent outbursts, and her episodes of disregard for the safety of others and herself create a chaotic situation that has forced her into an institutionalized state.

I find that those institutions are at a loss for how to address her situation. The months have dragged on with little or no communication from those in charge, other than to ask whether I will be her authorized representative to consent for her treatment when she bounces back to the hospital from the jail. Her memory lapses. I think about the possibility that Cara has something else going on medically, something more than a schizophrenia-type illness. Her habit of losing personal belongings and her failure to respond to medications has me wondering if Cara also has early-onset Alzheimer's disease.

The few and brief conversations I've had with Cara reveal that she remains paranoid, suspicious, and odd—even when she is undergoing treatment. A victim of anosognosia, she is unaware of her illness. But she seems aware that something is wrong, aware of what her illness has cost her: her freedom, her daughter, her life.

Cara, who is currently incarcerated, went back to court on May 30 of 2019, but the forensic assessment on sanity at the time of the offense was still not complete. Her case was continued until June 12. Stephen, Maria, and I were present for her court date, happy to at least see Cara's face and see that she was OK—even if we couldn't speak to her.

The entire day reminded us how her illness entrapped her within an immense bureaucracy that moves painfully slowly and often in inappropriate directions. She is doubly trapped: within her illness and the bureaucratic system. And she has missed so much—my mother's funeral, family trips, and reunions, and so many of Maria's milestones: learning to drive, getting her driver's license, college tours, family trips, and reunions. It's as if she is deceased, but still living; gone, but still here.

The same is true for so many who suffer from serious brain disorders. They are locked away to keep them and the community safe. But a locked door does not facilitate treatment. In fact, they only prolong decisionmaking and the overall treatment process since court orders are required at every turn.

The day of Cara's court date, we arrived at the courthouse early, afraid that we might miss her case being called. We sat while other cases were heard by the judge. I had the strong sense that many of the individuals in court that day were there because of mental illness.

The bailiff called the next case on the docket.

"The court now calls Janice Thomas."

A tall woman with tousled hair dressed in blue-gray hospital garb walked into the courtroom and was sworn in.

"Do you promise to tell the truth, the whole truth, and nothing but the truth?" The bailiff asked.

"I do," the woman responded in a clear and warm voice.

"Ms. Thomas, are you currently hospitalized at Jefferson County Manor?"

"Yes," she responded.

"Under what circumstances were you hospitalized at Jefferson County Manor?"

"I tried to kill myself by taking all of my medication," she responded quietly.

"Do you still want to kill yourself, Ms. Thomas?"

"No. I do not. I don't want to die any longer. I realize that my children need me, and I could never do that to them. Dr. Johnson said that I can go home today."

"Nothing further, your Honor." The public defender rested his case and was followed by the prosecuting attorney.

"Ms. Thomas, do you still feel that you are being followed?"

Ms. Thomas responded. "I have never felt that I was being followed."

"You have never felt that paparazzi were following you?" the prosecutor countered.

"Well, at one time, there were paparazzi."

"There were paparazzi. Do you still feel like the paparazzi are looking for you?" asked the prosecuting attorney.

"No. I misspoke. There were no paparazzi."

"Ms. Thomas, you just mentioned paparazzi. What were you referring to?"

"I didn't mean to say paparazzi. I misspoke," Ms. Thomas repeated.

"The prosecution rests, your Honor."

The judge looked at the computer screen, appearing to read notes on the case, and made his ruling.

"Ms. Thomas, the court requires that you remain for further treatment at Jefferson County Manor. That will give you a little longer to work with the doctors there."

And then they called the next case… it went on like this for hours.

As we waited, we were reminded how bound mental health and the justice system are, since mental illness affects the legal situation of most of the cases heard. Sadly, the destructive power of mental illness has no bounds—it seems like it's everywhere you look. Wherever there are people suffering, mental illness appears to be lurking in the shadows.

My family and I watched as the lawyers shuffled through their stacks of papers and the judge scrolled through computer files while the fates of real people were held in the balance. It was as though the beating heart of humanity was lost in a process of legal wrangling.

Finally, Cara's case was called. She came out looking almost childlike in her orange jumpsuit, her face framed by long curly hair and devoid of makeup. We couldn't talk to her, only look at her through our tears. She seemed pleased to see us. Just a glimpse of her was worth the trip to Jefferson County.

The moment felt extremely brief; they continued her case. It felt as though we'd showed up for nothing. She looked extremely scared as she was taken away again. It distressed me how inhumane the whole process was, treating my poor sister like a criminal. Later, we went to see the building that had caught fire. It had a big metal fence around it. Of course, the firefighter had been trying to protect Cara, but society can't comprehend a situation like my sister's, where someone is so sick that something like a massive fire doesn't exist in their mind; they're existing in a different reality.

I can only wonder what the end point will be, knowing that Cara's illness will likely get worse over time, as these illnesses do. I hope for a compassionate and appropriate clinical plan for her, but I know that these institutions provide far less. I know that she needs a group home, a case manager, and ongoing supervision, but unfortunately, I suspect she will be provided with much, much less. These institutions fail people time and time again, too often resulting in deadly consequences for those who are ill and others around them. Her illness is getting worse and more dangerous, and I worry that those who are making decisions will not see this oncoming train. These same jails and hospitals are overcrowded and overwhelmed, and I suspect that Cara's case will get lost in the endless shuffle.

I ask myself: will she be convicted and spend more time in jail? Will she be granted a not guilty by reason of insanity (NGRI) status, which will result in much more time in a psychiatric hospital, or will she be released with time served? The minimum sentence of one year for a class 6 felony is approaching.

I know what she needs, but these intuitions don't seem to have a clue. Or, they know and don't provide it. They fail to care adequately for individuals with brain disorders, among other impairments. Cara has gone months without treatment for her diabetes and high blood pressure. Is this the best we can do? Throw individuals who are ill in jail after they commit a crime in their confused state that you'd have to be blind to not see coming? When ill, Cara is dangerous, and she will hurt herself and others in her confused state. Does she belong in jail?

It appears that, as sophisticated as our society is, we are not yet ready—or prepared—to truly care for people like Cara.

Stephen and I awaken each morning to Cara's car and belongings in our garage, her daughter nestled in her bedroom—Cara's life broken into pieces that we oversee. They have her body, and we have everything else. Yet, we know next to nothing about what her destiny will be. We can only hope and pray as we prepare for the upcoming court date.

And now, after a felony charge for punching a firefighter while psychotic, Cara has spent almost an entire year between the regional jail and a psychiatric hospital.

I have a hard time finding her as she is moved back and forth between the jail and the state hospital (the criminal and civil side of "psychiatric institutionalization"). My sense is that Cara's attorney is trying to have her found not guilty by reason of insanity (NGRI) so that she won't have a felony conviction. This is noble on his part. However, in Virginia, if she is deemed NGRI, she will spend an average of three years in a psychiatric hospital. She still will not receive the needed neurological work-up for normal pressure hydrocephalus.

The quality of psychiatric care in the state hospital is marginal at best. Cara could very well have the same disorder as our mother. She has all the symptoms. Rather than rule out the likely cause for Cara's symptoms, a buildup of cerebrospinal fluid, she will likely be locked away in a hospital for years and prescribed the same antipsychotics that have not worked and that subsequently resulted in her punching a firefighter.

I feel defeated after 25 years of struggling with my family's unrelenting illnesses without seeing any success. Despite years of psychiatric treatment, there is no improvement. She's ill more than not. She is always paranoid, suspicious of my, as well as others', actions to help her.

Still, I try to keep up with Cara's whereabouts. I call her regularly to check on her. She, on the other hand, makes no effort to contact me or Maria, her only daughter, whom Stephen and I are raising. I hear nothing but anger and disdain in her voice when I call. Sometimes, she accuses me of things.

"Why did you ask David and Sylvia to leave, whore?"

"Cara, you know I would never ask your friends to leave or not visit you."

"Why do you keep putting me in the hospital? Did you tell my lawyer to keep me here?"

I often feel provoked to the point of lashing out, but I remember it's the illness that causes her to behave this way. This is not the real Cara. But I never know which Cara I will encounter when I reach out to her. Two weeks ago, Cara had me speak to her treatment team, but then yesterday, she attacked me viciously and told me that she didn't want me as her authorized representative. Her paranoia fluctuates, and I go from being her helpful sister to the worst person on earth.

Stephen and I have spent years trying to save Cara from my mother's fate. Perhaps she has schizoaffective disorder, bipolar type. Or, perhaps she has normal pressure hydrocephalus. My mother carried the diagnosis of schizoaffective disorder for most of her life, only to be diagnosed with normal pressure hydrocephalus in her 60s. I can't get a doctor to examine Cara for the disorder.

Cara's is another case of stigma around mental illness standing in the way of proper medical treatment. Her diabetes is extremely high, but the doctors don't give her insulin; it's as if they're waiting for her to die. She had a stroke, and her face and arms were paralyzed on one side, but still, they didn't admit her to the hospital or run scans. How is that ethical? She's a veteran and can go to the VA, but they barely do anything to help her. It's worse than being a second-class citizen.

11

AT OUR CHILDREN'S DOOR: LESSONS LEARNED FROM PREVIOUS GENERATIONS

"There are those who say 'Life dealt you a hand of cards and you ain't gonna get no more. And it all depends on how you play it:' I've worked on a theory that would say… there is a way to beat nature's card game… to beat the dealer… if you know enough about the system. You don't have to be a pawn of the system."

–Bowen, 1984

Maria sat motionless in the dark. Staring ahead, her hair uncombed, wearing clothes from the day prior. She had a secret that none of us could really fathom. Moments prior, she had overdosed on Tylenol and Ibuprofen, cut her wrists, and was awaiting death.

On the morning of Maria's suicide attempt, I opened her

bedroom door to wish her good morning, as I normally do. This morning, I was concerned though as she had recently lost her two best friends to a misunderstanding.

"Good morning! How are you feeling?" I asked.

"I'm fine." She responded in a loud, angry voice very much unlike her.

Her tone shocked me, as it was much like her mother Cara's tone when she is angry and psychotic.

"Let me know if you want to talk." I said, as I slowly closed the door, frightened for her, frightened for us.

"What does this mean?" I worried about what to do. Maria had seen her therapist the evening before. I later found out from Maria that the family session hadn't gone well, in her opinion. We first met with the therapist as a family, and afterwards, Maria met with him individually. Things appeared alright afterwards, but Maria later explained that she didn't feel supported by me and my husband during the session. That left her feeling even more abandoned and alone with her pain and loss.

After speaking to Maria, I looked for Stephen and told him that I was worried about her.

"Do you think she is suicidal?" I asked for the second time. I'd asked Maria this question yesterday at the therapist's office, and she'd responded with an emphatic "no." At the time, I felt embarrassed for asking—like I was overreacting. I had a vague nagging feeling, though.

Stephen and I, both tired from the long therapy session yesterday evening and the constant family drama, just wanted to rest—to have one moment of peace. I hoped it would all blow over—Maria would make new friends, and we would work through any misunderstandings we had as a family.

Maria did not afford us the opportunity.

The night passed. The next morning, I checked on Maria. She appeared groggy but indicated once again that she was fine. I was worried but went to work as planned. Stephen worked from home and was there for Maria. He and Maria were very close. Later in the day, Stephen said Maria came to him and said:

"I think I need to go to the hospital."

"What makes you think that?" Stephen asked.

"I cut myself."

Maria showed Stephen her arms. Both had numerous superficial cuts. She next led him to her room, where she showed him a kitchen knife stained with dried blood.

Stephen drove Maria to the emergency room. They sat mostly in silence during the drive to the hospital as Stephen pondered why she didn't come to him prior to harming herself, and Maria sat without a word, fixed gaze, appearing lost.

Maria was assessed immediately and admitted to the triage nurse that she was suicidal, told her about cutting her arms as well as taking large doses of Tylenol and Ibuprofen.

Maria was assessed by a psychiatrist and psychologist, and it was determined that she needed to be admitted to an adolescent unit at a nearby psychiatric hospital. The decision was made rather quickly. The system appeared ready to receive her, but finding a bed took almost a day. Many hours later, when the shift was changing, the triage nurse responded to the nurse taking over her care:

"Oh, this is SI here in number 5."

The hospital staff had their own code to refer to those with suicidal ideation. Maria did not appear upset by any of it. Rather, she appeared relieved. Nor did she appear the least bit ambivalent about being hospitalized. She appeared comforted by going to the hospital—it seemed to be her goal to be admitted to a psychiatric hospital. Later, it was apparent that Maria felt the need to pay a price.

It had been almost a year since Maria last spoke to her mother. She referred to us as her mother and father. She rarely mentioned Cara.

When Maria's friends abandoned her, as she abandoned her own mother, she felt a deep troubling sorrow. Filled with guilt and despair, she attempted to take her own life. She sat in the dark room tearing at her skin—punishing herself for an imagined crime. Maria had done nothing wrong. She was trying to survive under cruel circumstances. The world isn't always fair, and we can only cope as best we can.

It was as if Maria went to find her mother at the hospital. Sorry she abandoned her mother, she suddenly wanted to know more about her mother's condition, her mother's experiences, and she was sorry... She appeared so very sorry.

It appeared that Maria wanted to atone for her mistreatment of her mother and even more to explore what her mother had experienced so many times. And she got her chance. Maria was hospitalized for two weeks. She wanted to stay at the hospital longer. Somehow, being at the hospital helped Maria feel closer to her mother, who had been hospitalized against her will for over a year. Cara had been found not guilty by reason of insanity (NGRI).

Maria was diagnosed with major depression, single episode, severe. She was prescribed Depakote by the child and adolescent psychiatrist. And later Latuda. Fortunately, and because of our family's experiences taking antidepressants, Maria was not given any antidepressants that would have likely made her condition worse by triggering a manic episode. Maria recovered from the depression, made new friends, finished her senior year with a 3.9 grade point average, and was accepted to four universities.

Maria didn't run from the illness as my mother and siblings did, and as Cara still does. Maria embraced the illness. She had a desire to know more… to do things differently. And, she does do things differently. She manages the illness rather than the illness managing her.

These multigenerational issues are passed through the generations. They cut through the generations like an arctic icebreaker ship. They loom over the unaware, the naïve who don't know that the template for their destiny is written. It's through awareness and learning about your family that one can move beyond the potholes and be prepared for what may come.

12

FROM SADNESS TO MADNESS: THE CAREGIVER'S FATE

A great challenge for anyone who has lost a loved one to illness is to cope with their potential suffering and eventual death. When one's loved one is diagnosed with a mental illness, their suffering is almost certain, but rarely is their death from the mental illness. Rather, the loved one is sane at times and then insane—it's as if they are there one minute and gone the next. Family members of those diagnosed with mental illnesses struggle with ambiguous grief. There is no end to the grieving.

Both the caregiver and the mentally ill languish in a fog, not able to find each other—not able to connect through the fog of mental illness. When they do connect, there is a celebration that eventually ends in despair. The celebration doesn't endure as their loved one returns to insanity.

In families, we internalize our loved ones and carry them with us. We may think of them daily, consciously or subconsciously. They are always with us. We wonder what our loved one is thinking, what they might say, or how they would react to things we see and do day to day. Inevitably realizing they aren't there, and they can't be. The mental illness always seems to take them back. Grief, remorse, and loss again and again…

If this drags on long enough, the depths of despair can become inescapable, along with the inevitable trauma and anger. Eventually, the exhausted caregiver can be lost in a sea of despair. It just drags on and on.

I try to make peace with it. I pray as my grandmother taught me to do—looking for blessings in disguise. I may even try to find some fairness in it, desperately trying to level the playing field. But in the end, that playing field remains a wondrous, painful, and brutal place where wins and losses are a part of whatever this "game" is. We struggle to discern the rules of the game as we play on, hoping to move the ball without getting knocked to the ground, injured… or worse.

13

FORGIVENESS: LETTING GO AT LAST

If you give up when it's deep winter,
you'll surely miss the promise of your Spring,
the beauty of your Summer
and the fulfillment of your Fall.

Don't let the pains of one season
overshadow the joys of the rest of the year.
Try not to judge life
by one difficult season;
cherish instead
the exceptional seasons
given you in love

–Parable of the Pear Tree, n.d.

My mother passed away on December 20, 2018. The official cause of death: cerebral atherosclerosis and normal pressure hydrocephalus.

I was in charge of her obituary, but I couldn't use a picture of her from her older years. Instead, I chose a photograph from when she was young and beautiful. My mother had always been extremely vain, and getting older was very difficult for her. To her, everything had to be perfect, even though it was so not perfect.

Before her funeral, I sat at my desk, trying to write my mother's memorial.

"Stephen, I can't think of anything nice to say about my mother."

"It will come," Stephen replied.

"I'm not so sure about that. How do you say something nice about someone who was so mean and cut off from everyone?"

"It will come."

Clearly, Stephen had more faith in me than I had in myself!

"I love you, Stephen."

The day of my mother's funeral, I rehearsed the speech that I had prepared. I had my reservations. How do I tell the truth and still provide comfort to those present? Part of me was still angry from the years of abuse that I'd endured, from my childhood that was pure insanity day in and day out.

I was back at the family church 50 years later, the same church where I'd witnessed the Holy Ghost enter those bodies so many decades ago.

I walked to the podium, still uncertain of my words. I took my mother's memorial from my pocket, unfolded it, and began to read the words that I had carefully drafted. I looked up from my prepared speech, out over my family and friends. Perhaps the Holy Ghost entered me in that moment. I felt myself letting go of my rage and bitterness as I finally grieved the unfathomable—that the people who were supposed to love me had in fact done me great harm.

As so many of us do, I had survived horrendous and barbaric experiences in my family. While studying to become a therapist and honing my skills for over 30 years, I had considered my family's as well as others' often destructive actions and conceptualized countless cases. I had examined my wounds and worked with many therapists.

Yet, I couldn't let go of my rage. I couldn't stop engaging in cognitive distortions of perfectionism and negative self-talk, self-shaming, and apologizing for my very existence. For many years, I failed to be assertive, set boundaries, and act in the moment to protect myself from bullies. I continued to scan the environment for perceived dangers and hide from them. I've learned that hiding never works. Bullies and individuals with predatory behaviors always smell those who are weakest and pursue them. I continue to work on being assertive.

However, after my mother's death, I was able to let go of my rage. I let go of that hurt and many others as I truly came to understand how flawed humans are, and yet, how beautiful our love for each other can be.

I began to cry up there at the podium as I realized how much I loved them all—how much I loved my mother and how fortunate I was to have this enormous, extremely flawed family. With tear-filled eyes, I tried to read what I had so carefully composed, but I couldn't see the words. Instead, I closed my notes, placed them back in my pocket, and spoke these words:

"My mother was ill for many years. In illness, my mother would be confused at times. Those who knew my mother prior to her illness know that she had a gentle spirit. I learned many things from my mother, but what I learned most of all was love for family. My mother spent many hours daily speaking to each of you. She was always reaching out to family and friends... a rarity. She loved you all, and I love you. Thank you for the support you have given our family throughout the years."

All the years of rage simply dissolved. I was filled with the peace that I had been seeking for so long. I did love them. Forgiveness was not needed, just deliverance.

But I still have a lot of work to do. Every day, I encounter triggers that I react to in ways that drop my mood or cause intense anxiety. I struggle with viewing life through damaged lenses, but I work towards getting better every day.

14

WHAT LIVES IN THE DARKNESS WILL COME TO LIGHT

"Physician help thyself;
thus, you help your patients too.
Let this be his best – that he,
the patient, may behold with his eyes
the man who heals himself"

–Nietzsche, 1885, p. 2

There is power in adversity. With adversity comes challenge and discomfort. As people, we have the power to decide how we respond to events that are challenging. Therefore, adversity can be positive or negative. It can wound until we learn to channel our thoughts regarding what may be very painful circumstances.

Additionally, each of us reacts and behaves according to what we believe is happening around us. Each of us has our own reality.

Our past sets us up for how we will behave and react; we develop learned behaviors. The past becomes a wallpaper for our present reality.

Our sense of reality comes from our five senses—how we take information in and process it. Some of us have a sense of reality that is far afield of others. So, how do we make it in a world where each person has his or her own sense of reality and their own past? And how do we cope with the actions of those who feel justified in doing harm, because they are operating from within a different reality?

I am haunted by images and sounds from my past that affect my reality. The horrifying beatings inflicted upon my mother, the sounds of my mother's screams, breaking and overturned furniture, Biyo's savage death at the hands of my father, Danny's cries… and more difficult is rejecting the cognitive distortions that I carry from childhood. The normalization of the brutality, the inconsistent messages around morality, the negative characteristics assigned to me (*ugly, stupid, bad*), the shaming and constant comparison to others that left deep scars scorched onto my soul.

Looking back, I wonder how I could not know that my family's everyday reality was more than a little askew. Who breaks a chair over their partner's back? Who smothers a baby to stop him from crying? Who beats their dog with a garden hose? Who races down city streets, running stops signs, sending their car airborne while transporting their wife and three young children? Who laughs, as my mother did, during these manic drives as if having the time of her life?

Was my childhood reality so different from others'? Now I wonder… I always assumed that people are inherently good, and that my family was very different from other families and extremely flawed. Now, I struggle with my perception that many people are not inherently good.

Perhaps my genetics save me from the psychosis that afflicted everyone in my immediate family. Although, to them, I had lost the genetic lottery with my dark skin and black features, perhaps I was being saved from an even darker reality.

I think about what my life would look like if I hadn't gone to college or if I'd moved back home to take care of my mother after my father died. Yes, perhaps my mother's life would have been different, maybe better—but where would I be? I wouldn't have five degrees and be married to my husband living a life that I love. I would have nothing. I would be the scapegoat of the family, and they would be happily ever after.

Stephen and I have spent many years of our lives supporting my family members, trying to help, and grieving our ultimate failure to make much of a difference. It's hard to describe the anguish, unrelenting sadness, fear, and horror that follows every incident. It seems to never end. We barely get a break from one crisis only to be faced with another.

But many of the efforts—ours and the doctors'—are at best "Band-Aids." Every time a family member is detained to a psychiatric hospital, the doctors prescribe medication, but they don't conduct brain scans or physical examinations. It's like they are putting tape on a broken chair leg, selling the chair to an unsuspecting buyer who leaves the store believing they can sit in the chair. Of course, the buyer of the chair, like the psychiatric patient, crashes to the ground within a short period of time.

Somehow, I still have hope that Cara can be helped. Schizophrenia, hydrocephalus, Alzheimer's... What's the connection? If only someone could find a cure. My family needs a cure for this brain disorder, or are there multiple disorders at work here?

I had a private autopsy conducted on my mother, hoping to get answers that might help Cara's doctors and inform her care. My mother and Cara's symptoms seem so similar, and their illnesses present the same, but the findings from the autopsy shocked me. My mother, who had been diagnosed with schizoaffective disorder and normal pressure hydrocephalus, was now diagnosed with Alzheimer's disease. In fact, it was determined to be the cause of her death. I felt overwhelmed by the autopsy findings, and then numb. How was this information going to help Cara?

At least we can be there for Maria. Neither I, nor Stephen, wanted to start over again raising a child. In fact, I cried. I was 48 years old; I was tired! Our son was grown, but still depended on us for financial and emotional support. He had been an ill child, and it was tough meeting his needs. I felt too worn out to raise a child. So did Stephen.

But we loved Maria and couldn't imagine anyone else raising her. I love her even more today. I didn't think it was possible to love someone else's biological child as much as your own. I was wrong.

I am blessed to have an amazing partner in my husband who tells me that he loves me daily. I feel unconditionally loved. I know how fortunate I am to have this. His companionship and love have made a huge difference in my life. No matter what conditions I encounter outside of our home, I am guaranteed peace and tranquility when I return to our "nest."

Much of my happiness has grown from the stable and loving life that Stephen and I have created together. We've worked very hard for what we have: a nice home, a healthy environment for our son, the ability to take trips and enjoy our time together. It hasn't always been easy to keep our lives on track; over the years, it has seemed like, every time something good happens, something crazy happens in turn with my family. But I'm proud of what we've been able to achieve together.

My husband is there for me, and I am there for him. It makes all the difference in the world—having a sanctuary to return to at the end of the day. It's important to create environments that are nurturing for you and your loved ones, as much as you can. We do what we can to create positive environments, but it is best that we develop an inner sanctuary that we can carry with us wherever we go.

I learned that to heal and build my inner sanctuary, I must examine what has been buried in my subconscious. Anger and hurt can fester and control behavior in ways that most cannot imagine. And what is buried in our subconscious can dictate the makeup of our identity, for better or worse. Coming to terms with what is buried in the subconscious can help forge a stronger identity for the future. The ideal is to become stronger and more resilient.

Developing an inner sanctuary can be accomplished in a variety of ways. This is unique to each of us. I am slowly learning to do this. Building my inner sanctuary means cultivating the positive, integrating lessons learned and building my toolbox of adaptive behaviors. But foremost, it means establishing my identity: knowing myself and having boundaries. My identity is no longer up for grabs.

My upbringing was hard, but it doesn't define me. We live in an imperfectly perfect world where bad and good happen, often simultaneously. Change is the only thing that is guaranteed. Each moment brings something new. For now, I have the unconditional support of my husband, his embrace, his gentle kisses, his warm hands. Nothing lasts forever in the same way, and neither will we. How do we accept the pain that will inevitably come… the pain that life promises?

I hold my husband closer knowing that we won't be together forever. I believe that I will see him again in Heaven but am uncertain as to what the nature of our relationship will be then. It's easy to say that we will be together again, but in what manner will we be together? Stephen will always be a part of me, just like my parents. I am certain that I will choose to hold his memory closest. My imperfect past makes my present that much more perfect.

I am not a physician, but I am a psychotherapist. I don't have any grand answers or solutions to the pains of life. But I have survived traumatic events and live with chronic sorrow. My childhood left me with a weak sense of identity. What do you do when your identity is up for grabs? For a long while, it may have helped me survive abuse and the roller coaster ride of each family member succumbing to illness.

I desire something more now. I believe having unconditional regard in a stable and consistent partner through the journey of healing is paramount. If one is lucky enough to have that support naturally, *terrific*! If not, try finding a therapist that can accompany you on your journey. One size does not fit all. Don't be discouraged if it takes time to find the right therapist for you. Keep trying.

I look to the little things that lift my spirits. I see the swallows that dart around the yard in the spring. I watch the robins as they work so hard at building nests for their pale blue eggs. I gaze at the blue sky that never looks quite the same from day to blessed day. I gaze into the faces of my children as they look to me to guide them and lift them up when they are having bad days. I close my eyes and remember what makes me smile—the feel of Stephen's hair, our embrace, a sun-filled day, puppy kisses… I think back to the summers that I spent with my grandmother and my time in church watching members of the congregation swell with the Holy Spirit.

In the end, I believe we are of God. The energy that is of God has been given to us. We are connected to a greater source. We are inseparable from God in that way—God is always with us, and we are always with Him.

REFERENCES

Arthur Schopenhauer Quotes. (n.d.). Retrieved January 30, 2019, from https://www.brainyquote.com/quotes/arthur_schopenhauer_104802

Bowen, Murray. (1984). Georgetown Clinical Conference Videotape with Victoria Harrison. Retrieved March 31, 2020, from: https://www.csnsf.org/

Cefai, Emmanuel (n.d.). Alone in Thought, Alone. Retrieved February 17, 2019, from https://www.poemhunter.com/poem/alone-in-grief-alone-in-thought-alone/

Dalberg, John. (1887). Acton-Creighton Correspondence. Retrieved January 3, 2019, from https://oll.libertyfund.org/quotes/214

Frost, Robert. (1920). Mountain Interval. New York: Henry Holt and Company. Retrieved April 27, 2019, from www.bartleby.com/119/

Kysely, C. A. (2010, December 21). What Is Real? Retrieved 2019, from https://www.poemhunter.com/poem/what-is-real-12/

Nietzsche, Friedrich. (1885). Thus Spake Zarathustra. Retrieved May 31, 2019, from http://www.feedbooks.com

Scott, E. (2011). *The Unwritten Rule.* New York: Simon Pulse.

www.ingramcontent.com/pod-product-compliance
Ingram Content Group UK Ltd.
Pitfield, Milton Keynes, MK11 3LW, UK
UKHW020423250726
13967UKWH00007B/2780